GET ORGANIZED

FOURTH EDITION

Ron Fry

Course Technology PTR

A part of Cengage Learning

COURSE TECHNOLOGY
CENGAGE Learning™

Australia, Brazil, Japan, Korea, Mexico, Singapore, Spain, United Kingdom, United States

COURSE TECHNOLOGY
CENGAGE Learning™

Get Organized, Fourth Edition
Ron Fry

**Publisher and General Manager,
Course Technology PTR:**
Stacy L. Hiquet

**Associate Director of
Marketing:**
Sarah Panella

Manager of Editorial Services:
Heather Talbot

Marketing Manager:
Mark Hughes

Senior Acquisitions Editor:
Mitzi Koontz

Interior Layout Tech:
Judy Littlefield

Cover Designer:
Luke Fletcher

Indexer:
Larry D. Sweazy

Proofreader:
Sandi Wilson

For product information and technology assistance, contact us at **Cengage Learning Customer & Sales Support, 1-800-354-9706**

For permission to use material from this text or product, submit all requests online at **cengage.com/permissions** Further permissions questions can be e-mailed to **permissionrequest@cengage.com**.

All trademarks are the property of their respective owners.

All images © Cengage Learning unless otherwise noted.

Library of Congress Control Number: 2011930894

ISBN-13: 978-1-4354-6114-7

ISBN-10: 1-4354-6114-2

Course Technology, a part of Cengage Learning
20 Channel Center Street
Boston, MA 02210
USA

Cengage Learning is a leading provider of customized learning solutions with office locations around the globe, including Singapore, the United Kingdom, Australia, Mexico, Brazil, and Japan. Locate your local office at: **international.cengage.com/region**.

Cengage Learning products are represented in Canada by Nelson Education, Ltd.

For your lifelong learning solutions, visit **courseptr.com**.

Visit our corporate Web site at **cengage.com**.

Printed by RR Donnelley.
Crawfordsville, IN. 1st Ptg. 06/2011

Printed in United States of America
1 2 3 4 5 6 7 13 12 11

Contents

STARTING AT THE BEGINNING

This marks another major milestone in the 20-year-long evolution of my *How to Study Program*—the reissuance of new editions of the key volumes: *How to Study* itself, now in a seventh edition; sixth editions of *Improve Your Memory, Improve Your Reading, Improve Your Writing,* and *"Ace" Any Test;* and a fourth edition of the book you're currently reading, *Get Organized.*

I am truly proud, though somewhat amazed, that these books are now moving into their third decade. While all authors want to believe their books will last forever, most wind up in the remainder bin far sooner than we would ever like (or admit).

Why You're Reading This Book

A number of you are students, not just the high school students I always thought were my readers, but also college students and, much to my delight, even *middle* school students (which says something quite positive about your ambition and what I anticipate will be your eventual success).

Many of you reading this are adults. Some of you are returning to school. And some of you are long out of school but have figured out that if you can learn *now* the study skills your teachers never taught you (or you never took the time to learn), you will do better in your careers—especially if you know how to meet pressing deadlines or organize the key points of a presentation.

All too many of you are parents with the same lament: "How do I get Johnny to do better in school? If his life is as organized as his room, I fear for all of us!"

If You're a High School Student

You should be particularly comfortable with both the language and format of this book—its relatively short sentences and paragraphs, occasionally humorous (hopefully) headings and subheadings, a reasonable but certainly not outrageous vocabulary. I wrote it with you in mind!

If You're a Middle School Student

Learning now how to organize your studying and your life is absolutely key to your future success. You are trying to learn how to study at precisely the right time. Sixth, seventh, and eighth grades—before that sometimes cosmic leap to high school—are without a doubt the period in which these study skills should be mastered. If you're serious enough about studying to be reading this book, I doubt you'll have trouble with the concepts or the language.

If You're a "Traditional" College Student

Having pretty much gone right from high school to college, learning how to organize your life and studies is not just a nice idea—it's the only thing that will enable you to survive. Trust me. You haven't even contemplated how busy life can be until you show up at old Klutzburg U. and get your first class schedule...and volunteer schedule... and athletics schedule...and work schedule.

If You're the Parent of a Student of Any Age

Your child's school is probably doing little, if anything, to teach him or her how to study. Which means he or she is not learning how to *learn*. And that means he or she is not learning how to *succeed*.

Should the schools be accomplishing that? Absolutely. After all, we spend more than $300 billion on elementary and secondary education in this country. We ought to be getting more for that money than a diploma, some football cheers, and a discouraging entry-level job market.

What Can Parents Do?

There are probably even more dedicated parents out there than dedicated students, since the first phone call at any of my radio or TV appearances comes from a sincere and worried parent asking, "What can I do to help my kid do better in school?" Okay, here they are, the rules for parents of students of any age:

1. **Set up a homework area.** Free of distraction, well lit, with all necessary supplies handy.

2. **Set up a homework routine.** When and where it gets done. Studies have clearly shown that students who establish a regular routine are better organized and, as a result, more successful.

3. **Set homework priorities.** Actually, just make the point that homework is the priority—before a date, before TV, before going out to play, whatever.

4. **Make reading a habit**—for them, certainly, but also for yourself. Kids will inevitably *do* what you do, not what you *say* (even if you say *not* to do what you *do*).

5. **Turn off the TV.** Or at the very least, severely limit when and how much TV-watching is appropriate. This may be the toughest suggestion to enforce. I know. I was once the parent of a teenager too.

6. **Talk to the teachers.** Find out what your kids are supposed to be learning. If you don't know the books they're supposed to be reading, what's expected of them in class, and how much homework they should be scheduling, you can't really give them the help they need.

7. **Encourage and motivate,** but don't nag them to do their homework. It doesn't work. The more you insist, the quicker they will tune you out.

8. **Supervise their work,** but don't fall into the trap of doing their homework. Proofreading a paper, for example, is a positive way to help your child in school. But if you simply put in corrections without your child learning from her mistakes, you're not helping her at all...except in the belief that she is not responsible for her own work.

9. **Praise them when they succeed,** but don't overpraise them for mediocre work. Kids know when you're being insincere and, again, will quickly tune you out.

10. **Convince them of reality.** (This is for older students.) Okay, I'll admit it's almost as much of a stretch as turning off the TV, but learning and believing that the real world will not care about their grades, but will measure them by what they know and what they can do, is a lesson that will save many tears (probably yours). It's probably never too early to (carefully) let your boy or girl genius get the message that life is not fair.

11. **If you can afford it, get your kid(s) a computer** and all the software they can handle. There really is no avoiding it: Your kids, what ever their ages, absolutely must be computer-savvy in order to survive in and after school.

12. **Turn off the TV already!**

13. **Get wired.** The Internet is the greatest invention of our age and an unbelievable tool for students of any age. It is impossible for a college student to succeed without the ability to surf the Internet, and nearly impossible for younger students as well. They've got to be connected.

14. But turn off IM (Instant Messaging) while doing homework. They will attempt to convince you that they can write their paper and do geometry and IM their friends at the same time. Parents who believe this have also been persuaded it's a fine idea to do homework in front of the TV.

The Importance of Your Involvement

The results of every study done in the last two decades about what affects a child's success in school clearly demonstrate that only one factor *overwhelmingly* affects it, every time: parental involvement—not the size of the school, the money spent per pupil, the number of language labs, how many of the students go on to college, how many great (or lousy) teachers there are. *None is as significant as the effect you can have.*

So please, take the time to read this book and find out what your kids *should* be learning. *You can help them, even if you were not a great student yourself, even if you never learned great study skills.* Learn with your child: Not only will it help him in school, it will help *you* on the job, whatever your field.

If You're a Nontraditional Student

If you're going back to high school, college, or graduate school at age 25, 45, 65, or 85, you probably need the help my books offer more than anyone! Why? Because the longer you've been out of school, the more likely you don't remember what you've forgotten. And you've probably forgotten what you're supposed to remember! As much as I emphasize that it's rarely too *early* to learn good study habits, I must also emphasize that it's never too *late*.

If you're returning to school and attempting to carry even a partial courseload while simultaneously holding down a job, raising a family, or both, there are some particular problems you probably didn't have to face the last time you were in school.

Time and money pressures. Let's face it: When all you had to worry about was going to school, it simply *had* to be easier than going to school, raising a family, and working for a living simultaneously. (And it was!) Mastering all of the techniques of time management is even more essential if you are to effectively juggle responsibilities to your career, family, clubs, and friends, in addition to your commitment to school. Money management may well be another essential skill, whether figuring out how to pay for child care (something you probably didn't have to worry about in high school) or how to manage all your responsibilities while cutting your hours at work to make time for school.

Self-imposed fears of inadequacy. You may convince yourself that you're just "out of practice" with all this school stuff. You don't even remember what to do with a highlighter! While some of this fear is valid, most is not.

Maybe you're worried because you didn't exactly light up the academic world the first time around. Well, neither did Edison or Einstein or a host of other successful people. But then, you've changed rather significantly since you were a kid, haven't you? Concentrate on how much *more* qualified you are for school *now* than you were *then*!

Feeling you're "out of your element." This is a slightly different fear, the fear that you just don't fit in anymore. After all, you're not 18 again. But then, neither are fully half the college students on campus today. That's right: Fully 50 percent of all college students are older than 25. The reality is, you'll probably feel more in your element now than you did the first time around!

You'll see teachers differently. Probably a plus. It's doubtful you'll exhibit the same level of awe you did the first time around. At worst, you'll consider teachers your equals. At best, you'll consider them younger and not necessarily as successful or experienced as you are. In either event, you probably won't be quite as ready to treat your college professors as if they were gods.

There are differences in academic life. It's slower than the "real" world, and you may well be moving significantly faster than its normal pace. When you were 18, an afternoon without classes meant time to hang out with friends. Now it might mean catching up on a week's worth of errands, cooking (and freezing) a week's worth of dinners, or writing four reports due this week. Despite your own hectic schedule, do not expect campus life to accelerate in response. You will have to get used to people and systems with far less interest in speed.

Some Random Thoughts About Learning

Learning shouldn't be painful and certainly doesn't have to be boring, though it's far too often both. However, it's not necessarily going to be wonderful and painless, either. Sometimes you actually have to work hard to figure something out or get a project done. That *is* reality.

It's also reality that everything isn't readily apparent or easily understandable. Confusion reigns. Tell yourself that's okay and learn how to get past it. Heck, if you actually think you understand everything you've read the first time through, you're kidding yourself. Learning something slowly doesn't mean there's something wrong with *you*. It may be a subject that virtually everybody learns slowly. Or a textbook that is simply incomprehensible.

A good student doesn't panic when he just doesn't "get" something immediately. He takes his time, follows whatever steps apply, and remains confident that the lightbulb of understanding will eventually glow.

Parents often ask me, "How can I motivate my teenager?" My initial response is usually to smile and say, "If I knew the answer to that question, I would have retired very wealthy quite some time ago." However, I think there *is* an answer, but it's not something *parents* can do—it's something the student has to decide: Are you going to spend the school day interested and alert or bored and resentful?

It's really that simple. Since you have to go to school anyway, why not develop the attitude that you might as well be active and learn as much as possible instead of being miserable? The difference between a C and an A or B for many students is, I firmly believe, merely a matter of wanting to do better. As I constantly stress in radio and TV interviews, inevitably you will leave school. And very quickly, you'll discover that suddenly all anyone cares about is what you *know* and what you can *do*. Grades won't count anymore; neither will tests. So you can learn it all now or regret it later.

How many times have you asked yourself, "Why am I even trying to learn this calculus (algebra, geometry, physics, chemistry, history, whatever)? I'll *never* use it again!" Well, you really have *no clue* what you're going to need to know tomorrow or next week, let alone next year or next decade.

I've been amazed in my own life how things I did with no specific purpose in mind (except probably to earn money or meet a girl) turned out years later to be not just invaluable to my life or career, but essential. How was I to know when I took German as my language elective in high school that the most important international trade show in book publishing was in Frankfurt, Germany? Or that the basic skills I learned one year working for an accountant (while I was writing my first book) would become essential when I later started four companies? Or how important basic math skills would be in selling and negotiating over the years? (Okay, I'll admit it: I haven't used a differential equation in 30 years, but, hey, you never know!)

So learn it *all*. And don't be surprised if the subject you'd vote "Least likely to ever be useful" winds up being the key to *your* fame and fortune.

You Don't Have to Do It "My Way"

Though I immodestly maintain that my *How to Study Program* is the most helpful to the most people, there are certainly plenty of other purported study books out there. Inevitably, these other books promote the authors' "system," which usually means what they did to get through school. This "system," whether basic and traditional or wildly quirky, may or may not work for you. So what do you do if "their" way of taking notes makes no sense to you? Or you master their highfalutin' "Super Student Study Symbols" and still get Cs?

There are very few "rights" and "wrongs" out there in the study world. There's certainly no single "right" way to attack a multiple choice test or take notes. So don't get fooled into thinking there *is*, especially if what you're doing seems to be working for you.

Don't change what "ain't broke" just because some self-proclaimed study guru claims what you're doing is all wet. Maybe he's all wet. After all, if his system works for you, all it *really* means is you have the same likes, dislikes, talents, or skills as the author.

Needless to say, don't read *my* books looking for that single, inestimable system of "rules" that works for everyone. You won't find it, 'cause there's no such bird.

You will find a plethora of techniques, tips, tricks, gimmicks, and what-have-you, some or all of which may work for you, some of which won't. Pick and choose, change and adapt, figure out what works for you. Because *you* are the one responsible for creating *your* study system, *not me*.

I've used the phrase "Study smarter, not harder" in promotion and publicity for the *How to Study Program* for more than 20 years. Does that mean I guarantee you'll spend less time studying? Or that the least amount of time you can study is best? Or that studying isn't ever supposed to be hard?

Hardly. It does mean that studying inefficiently is wasting time that could be spent doing other (okay, probably more *fun*) things and that getting your studying done as quickly and efficiently as possible is a realistic, worthy, and *attainable* goal. I'm no stranger to hard work, but I'm not a monastic dropout who thrives on self-flagellation. I try not to work harder than I have to!

I Repeat: Get Wired

In 1988, when I wrote the first edition of *How to Study,* I composed it, formatted it, and printed it on (gasp) a personal computer. Most people did *not* have a computer, let alone a neighborhood network and DSL, or surf the Internet (whatever that was,) or chat online, or Instant Message their friends, or...you get the point.

In case you've been living in a cave that doesn't have Wi-Fi, those days are dead and gone. And you should cheer, even if you aren't sure what DOS was (is? could be?). Because the spread of the personal computer and, even more important, the Internet, has taken studying from the Dark Ages to the Info Age in a remarkably short time.

As a result, you will find all of my books assume you have a computer and know how to use it—for note taking, reading, writing papers, researching, and much more. There are many tasks that may be harder on a computer— and I'll point them out—but don't believe for a second that a computer won't help you tremendously, whatever your age, whatever your grades.

As for the Internet, it has absolutely revolutionized research. Whether you're writing a paper, putting together a reading list, studying for the SAT, or just trying to organize your life, it has become a more valuable tool than the greatest library in the world. Heck, it *is* the greatest library in the world...and more. So if you are not Internet-savvy (yes, I'm talking to the parents out there, couldn't you tell?), admit you're a technology dummy, get a book (via the Internet, of course), and get online! You'll be missing far too much—and be studying far harder—without it.

A Couple of Final Points

I believe in gender equality, but often find constructions such as "he and she," "s/he," "womyn," and other such stretches to be painfully awkward. I have therefore attempted to sprinkle pronouns of both genders throughout the text.

Second, you will find that many similar pieces of advice, examples, lists, and other words, phrases, and sections appear in several of my books. This is unavoidable since many of you, despite my entreaties, will buy the one or two books you absolutely need and never see the others. So, if the same pertinent information must be included in three books, it will be. Forgive me the redundancy.

That said, I can guarantee that the nearly 1,000 pages of my *How to Study Program* contain the most wide-ranging, comprehensive, and complete system of studying ever published. I have attempted to create a system that is usable, useful, practical, learnable, flexible, and adaptable. One that *you* can use—whatever your age, whatever your level of achievement, whatever your IQ—to start doing better in school, in work, and in life *immediately*.

Good luck.

Ron Fry

CHAPTER 1

THE NEED FOR
ORGANIZATION

"Those who make the worst use of their time
are the first to complain of its brevity."
—La Bruyere (1688)

W hether you're a high school student just starting to feel frazzled; a college student juggling five classes and a part-time job; or a parent working, attending classes, and raising a family, a simple, easy-to-follow system of organization is crucial to your success. Despite your insistence that you just don't have the time to spend scheduling, listing, and recording, it's actually the best way to give yourself more time.

Taking Time To Make Time

I'm sure many of you reading this are struggling with some-times overwhelming responsibilities and commitments. Some of you may be so burned out that you've just given up. Those of you who aren't probably figure it's your fault—if you just worked harder, spent more time on your papers and assignments, wired yourself to your laptop 24/7—then everything would work out just fine.

So you resign yourselves to caffeine-fueled all-nighters, cramming for tests, and forgetting about time-consuming activities like eating and sleeping. Trying to do everything—even when there's too much to do— without acquiring the skills to *control* your time, is an approach that will surely lead to frustration and failure.

When Does It All End?

With classes, homework, a part- or full-time job, and so many opportunities for fun and recreation, life as a student can be very busy. But, believe me, it doesn't suddenly get easier when you graduate.

Most adults will tell you that life only gets busier. There will always be a boss who expects you to work later; children who need to be fed, clothed, and taken to the doctor; hob-bies and interests to pursue; community service to become involved in; courses to take; etc.

There May Not Be Enough Time for Everything

When I asked one busy student if she wished she had more time, she joked, "I'm glad there are only 24 hours in a day. Any more and I wouldn't have an excuse for not getting everything done!"

Let me give you the good news: There is a way that you can accomplish more in less time. And it doesn't take more effort. You can plan ahead and make conscious choices about how your time will be spent and how much time you will spend on each task. You can have more control over your time, rather than always running out of it.

Now the bad news: The first step to managing your time should be deciding just what is important...and what isn't. Difficult as it may be, sometimes it's necessary for us to recognize that we truly can't do it all, to slice from our busy schedules those activities that aren't that meaningful to us so we can devote more energy to those that are.

You may love music so much, you want to be in the school orchestra, jazz band, choir, and play with your own garage band on weekends. But is it realistic to commit to all four?

Your job at the mall boutique may mean you get 20 percent off all the clothes you buy there. But if you are working there 4 days a week, taking 15 hours of classes, and working at the food co-op on weekends, when do you expect to study?

If you're raising a family, working part-time, and trying to take a near-full class load yourself, it's probably time to cure yourself of the Super Mom syndrome.

But There Is Enough Time To Plan

Yet, even after paring down our commitments, most of us are still challenged to get it all done. What with classes, study time, work obligations, extracurricular activities, and a social life, it's not easy getting it all in.

The organizational plan that I outline in this book is designed particularly for students. Whether you're in high school, college, or graduate school, a "traditional" student or one who's chosen to return to school after being out in the "real world" for a while, you'll find that this is a manageable program that will work for you.

This program allows for flexibility. In fact, I encourage you to adapt any of my recommendations to your own unique needs. That means it will work for you whether you are living in a dorm, sharing accommodations with a roommate, or living with a spouse and children.

The purpose of this book is to help you make choices about what is important to you, set goals for yourself, organize and schedule your time, and develop the motivation and self-discipline to follow your schedule and reach those goals.

Wouldn't it be nice to actually have some *extra* time…instead of always wondering where it all went? To feel that you're exerting some control over your schedule, your schoolwork, your life…instead of caroming from appointment to appointment, class to class, assignment to assignment, like some crazed billiard ball?

It can happen.

I will not spend a lot of time trying to convince you that this is a "fun" idea—getting excited about calendars and to-do lists is a bit of a stretch. You will not wake up one morning and suddenly decide that organizing your life is just the most scintillating thing you can think of.

But I suspect you will do it if I can convince you that effective organization will reward you in some very tangible ways.

More Work, Less Time, More Fun!

An organizational or time-management system that fits your needs can help you get more work done in less time. Whether your priority is more free time, improved grades, a less frantic life—or all of the above—learning how to organize your life and your studies can help you reach your objective, because an effective time-management system:

1. **Helps you put first things first.** Have you ever spent an evening doing a time-consuming assignment for an easy class, only to find that you hadn't spend enough time studying for a crucial test in a more difficult one?

   Listing all of the tasks you are required to complete and *prioritizing* them ensures that the most important things will **always** get done—even on days when you don't get everything done.

2. **Helps you learn how long everything really takes.** One of the important components of this system is estimating how long each task will take you and tracking how long you actually spend doing it. Once you've inculcated this concept into your life, you'll finally discover where all that time you've been "losing" has been hiding.

3. **Reduces your tendency to procrastinate.** Once you have a realistic idea of the specific things you must accomplish and know that you have allocated sufficient time to do so, you're less likely to get frustrated and put them off.

4. **Helps you avoid time traps.** Time traps are the unplanned events that pop up, sometimes (it seems) every day. They're the fires you have to put out before you can turn to tasks like studying.

   You may fall into such time traps because they seem urgent...or because they seem fun. Or you may end up spending hours in them...without even realizing you're stuck.

   There is no way to avoid every time trap. But effective time management can help you avoid most of them. Time management is like a fire-*prevention* approach rather than a fire-*fighting* one: It allows you to go about your work systematically instead of moving from crisis to crisis or whim to whim.

5. Helps you anticipate opportunities. In addition to helping you balance study time with other time demands, effective time management can help make the time you do spend studying more productive. You'll be able to get more done in the same amount of time or—even better—do more work in less time. I'm sure you could find some way to spend those extra hours each week.

6. Gives you freedom and control. Contrary to many students' fears, time management is *liberating*, not restrictive. A certain control over *part* of your day allows you to be flexible with the *rest* of your day.

In addition, you will be able to plan more freedom into your schedule. For example, you would know well in advance that you have a big test the day after a friend's party. Instead of having to call your friend the night of the party with a big sob story, you could simply schedule sufficient study time a couple of days before the party. Then you could attend the party, enjoy yourself, and still ace that test the next day!

7. Helps you avoid time conflicts. Have you ever lived the following horror story? You get out of class at 5:30, remember you have a big math assignment due, then realize you have no time to do it since you have a music rehearsal at 6 p.m. Then you remember that your softball game is scheduled for 7 p.m....just before that date you made months ago (which you completely forgot about until you checked your voice mail).

Simply having all of your activities, assignments, appointments, errands, and reminders written down in one place helps ensure that two or three things don't get scheduled at once. If time conflicts do arise, you will notice them well in advance and be able to rearrange things accordingly.

8. **Helps you avoid feeling guilty.** When you know how much studying has to be done and have the time scheduled to do it, you can relax—you know that the work will get done. It is much easier to forget about studying if you've already allotted the time for it. Without a plan to finish the work you are doing, you may feel like it's "hanging over your head"— even when you're not working on it. If you're going to spend time thinking about studying, you might as well just spend the time studying!

Effective time management also helps keep your conscience off your back. When your studying is done, you can *really* enjoy your free time without feeling guilty because you're not studying.

9. **Helps you evaluate your progress.** If you know you have to read an average of 75 pages a week to keep up in your business management class, and you've only read 60 pages this week, you don't need a calculator to figure out that you are slightly behind. And it's easy enough to schedule a little more time to read next week so you can catch up.

On the other hand, if you only read when it doesn't cut into your leisure time (i.e., when your assignment doesn't conflict with your favorite TV programs) or until you're tired, you'll never know whether you're behind or ahead (but I'll bet you're behind!). Then one morning you suddenly realize you have to reach 150 pages of your history text...by lunchtime.

10. **Helps you see the big picture.** Effective time management provides you with a bird's-eye view of the semester. Instead of being caught off guard when the busy times come, you will be able to plan ahead—*weeks* ahead—when you have big tests or assignments due in more than one class. Why not complete that German culture paper a few days early so it's not in the way when two other papers are due...or you're trying to get ready for a weekend ski trip? Conflicts can be eliminated easily if you identify them in advance.

11. **Helps you see the bigger picture.** Planning ahead and plotting your course early allows you to see how classes fit with your overall school career. For example, if you know you have to take chemistry, biology, and pharmacology to be eligible for entrance into the nursing program, and the courses you will take later will build on those, you will at least be able to see why the classes are required for your major, even if you aren't particularly fond of one or two of them.

12. Helps you learn how to study smarter, not
harder. Students sometimes think time management just means reallocating their time—spending the same time studying, the same time in class, the same time partying, just shifting around these time segments so everything is more "organized."

This is only partially true—a key part of effective time management is learning how to prioritize tasks. But this simple view ignores one great benefit of taking control of your time: It may well be possible that you will be so organized, so prioritized, so in control of your time, that you can spend less time studying, get better grades, and have more time for other things—extracurricular activities, hobbies, whatever.

It's not magic, though it can appear magical.

It Keeps Getting Better

In addition to helping you to manage your time right now and reach your immediate study goals, learning how to organize your studying will continue to pay off.

Have you ever sat in a class and thought to yourself, "I'll *never* use this stuff once I get out of school"?

You won't say that about organizational skills. They will be useful throughout your life. Preparation is what school is all about—if you spend your time effectively now, you will be better prepared for the future.

And the better prepared you are, the more options you will have: Effective learning and good grades now will increase your range of choices when you graduate. The company you work for or the graduate school you attend will be one you choose, not one whose choice was dictated by poor past performance.

Learning how to manage your time now will develop habits and skills you can use outside of school. It may be difficult for you to develop the habits of effective time management, but don't think you're alone—time management presents just as much of a problem to many parents, professors, and nonstudents. How many people do you know who never worry about time?

If you learn effective time-management skills in school, the payoffs will come throughout your life.

Whether you wind up running a household or a business, you will have learned skills you will use every day.

Time management is not a magic wand that can be waved to solve problems in school or after graduation. It is a craft that must be developed over time. There is no "time-management gene" that you either have or lack, like the ones that produce brown eyes or black hair.

These techniques are tools that can be used to help you reach your short-term and long-range goals successfully.

The important thing to remember is that you can be a successful time manager and a successful student if you are willing to make the effort to learn and apply the principles in this book.

If you hate the idea of being tied to a schedule, if you fear that it will drain all spontaneity and fun from your life, I know you'll be pleasantly surprised when you discover that just the opposite is true.

Most students are relieved and excited when they learn what a liberating tool time management can be.

Let's explode some myths that may be holding you back.

Do I Have To Spend More Time Studying?

Learning effective organizational skills will not turn you into a study-bound bookworm. How much time do you need to set aside for studying? Ask your career counselor, and he or she will probably echo the timeworn 2:1 ratio—spend two hours studying *out* of class for every hour you spend *in* class.

Hogwash. That ratio may be way out of line—either not enough time or too much. The amount of study time you need to schedule depends on your classes, abilities, needs, and goals. It will undoubtedly differ from what your friends need to do.

Scheduling time to study doesn't mean that you have to go from three hours of studying a day to eight. In fact, laying out your study time in advance often means you can relax more when you're not studying because you won't be worrying about when you're going to get your schoolwork done—the time's been set aside.

How long you study is less important than how effective you are when you do sit down to study. The goal is not to spend more time studying, but to spend the same or less time, getting more done in whatever time you spend.

It's Too Complicated

You may fear that time management implies complexity. Actually, I recommend simplicity. The more complex your system, the harder it will be to use and, consequently, the less likely that you will use it consistently. The more complex the system, the more likely it will collapse.

It's Too Inflexible

You can design your time-management system to fit your own needs. Some of the skills you will learn in this book will be more helpful to you in reaching your goals than others. You may already be using some of them. Others you will want to start using right now. Still others may not fit your needs at all.

Use the skills that are most likely to lead you to your study goals, meet your needs, and fit with your personality.

Inflexibility is most people's biggest fear—"If I set it all out on a schedule, then I won't be able to be spontaneous and choose what to do with my time later."

Your time-management system can be as flexible as you want. In fact, the best systems act as guides, not some rigid set of "must do's" and "can't do's."

That's enough about the myths. Let's take a look at what is actually required to use your time-management skills effectively.

Keep It Together

You have to be able to look at your plan when it's time to use it. It's nearly impossible to make detailed plans very far in advance without having a permanent record. Make it your rule: "If I plan it out, I will write it down."

And make sure that you have *one place to write and keep all your schedule information*, including class times, meetings, study times, project due dates, vacations, doctor appointments, social events, etc., so you always know exactly where to find them.

Your Readiness To Adapt and Personalize

The time-management system that best suits you will be tailor-made to fit your needs and personality.

Consider the following example. Most parents turn the lights out and keep things quiet when their baby is trying to go to sleep. But I know of one baby who, after spending two months in the hustle and bustle of a newborn intensive-care unit, couldn't sleep unless the lights were *on* and it was *noisy*.

Similarly, while many students will study best in a quiet environment, others may feel uncomfortable without a radio blasting.

Make your study schedule work for you, not your night-owl roommate who must plan every activity down to the minute. Alter it, modify it, make it stricter, make it more flexible—whatever works for you.

You'll Never Be Disorganized Again!

We've all had the experience of missing an important appointment or commitment and saying, "I know I had that written down somewhere—I wonder *where?*"

It's easy to think, "I'll write it down so I won't forget," but a calendar or assignment book that is not used regularly isn't a safety net at all. You must consistently write down your commitments. You must spend time filling out your schedule every day, every week.

Any efforts you make to manage your time will be futile if you do not have your calendar with you when you need it. For example, you are in art class without it when your teacher reminds you your next project is due in a week. You jot it down in your art notebook and promise yourself you'll add it to your schedule as soon as you get home.

You hurry to your next class, and your geology instructor schedules a study session for the following week. You scribble a reminder in your lab book.

Between classes, a friend stops to invite you to a party Thursday night. You promise you'll be there. You tuck a note into your jeans.

You arrive at work to find out your supervisor has scheduled your hours for the following week. You commit to them.

Had you been carrying your calendar with you, you would have been able to write down when your art project was due and schedule the necessary amount of preparation time.

You would have realized that your geology study session was the same night as your friend's party and discovered that accepting the work schedule your supervisor presented left you with little time to work on your art project.

Take your PDA, planner, calendar, or assignment book with you anywhere and everywhere you think you might need it.

When In Doubt, Take It Along!

Keeping your calendar with you will reduce the number of times you have to say, "I'll just try to remember it for now" or "I'll write it down on this little piece of paper and transfer it to my planner later."

Always make a point of writing down tasks, assignments, phone numbers, and other bits of important information in your schedule immediately.

Use Your New System Consistently

In order to test its effectiveness, you must give any time-management system a chance to work—give it a trial run. No program can work unless it is utilized consistently. And consistency won't happen without effort.

It's just like learning to ride a bicycle. It's a pain at first; you may even fall down a few times. But once you're a two-wheel pro, you can travel much faster and farther than you could by foot.

The same goes for the techniques you will learn here— they may take practice and a little getting used to, but once you've lived a "reorganized" life for a couple of weeks, you'll probably find yourself in the habit of doing it. From then on, it will take relatively little effort to maintain.

That's when you'll really notice the payoff—when time management becomes second nature.

Chapter 2

Organize Your Life

In one of my favorite Abbott & Costello routines, the hapless Costello stands in front of a huge rolltop desk. There are hundreds—no, thousands—of papers spilling out of it. Suddenly, Abbott, the ultimate delegator, comes in and asks for "the Smerling contract, 1942." Costello pulls out a pair of enormous tongs, roots around in the cavernous desk, papers spilling everywhere, and pulls out a single sheet of paper. "Smerling contract, 1942," he blithely announces.

Many of us probably can boast of a "filing system" just as disorganized as Costello's, though I suspect more than a few (okay, me included) would contend that we really can find things in the clutter we like to call a desktop. Whether we're kidding ourselves or not, becoming more organized in our lives—whether we're students, homemakers, or career-ladder climbers—is key to succeeding in school, at home, and on the job.

Self-Quiz: What's Your Planning IQ?

To learn something about your present orientation to planning, take this quiz adapted from Jonathan and Susan Clark's *Make the Most of Your Workday* (Career Press, 1994), circling the answer that describes your orientation:

(3) agree   (2) not sure   (1) disagree.

I take regular time for planning every day.	3	2	1
I have a personally chosen calendar or organizational system.	3	2	1
I prioritize all my assignments daily.	3	2	1
I use a daily calendar.	3	2	1
I do not have difficulty making decisions.	3	2	1
I work daily on parts of projects due more than a week from now.	3	2	1
The gas tank in my car is presently at least half full.	3	2	1
I know exactly when my most productive time of day is.	3	2	1
I know my most important assignment for tomorrow.	3	2	1
I use a long-term planning calendar.	3	2	1

How did you do?

25 or more You have a plan, and are working it.

15 to 24 Sometimes your day gets the better of you.

Less than 15 How are you keeping up?

Why Things Don't Get Done

Are you frustrated at the end of the day? Is your to-do list nearly as long each evening as it was that morning? Do you sometimes feel you've spent all day busting your behind, but can rarely point to solid accomplishments? Nearly all productivity problems can be traced to one or more of the items on the following list.

▪ **No clear goals.** Without a specific sense of purpose, it's impossible to effectively manage and organize your priorities. You need to develop both a clear-cut, long-range goal and the short-term steps required to reach it. If you don't know where you're going, any road will take you there.

▪ **Lack of priorities.** The best to-do list ever written is useless if it hasn't been prioritized. Most people naturally work on the easy or fun things first. They may cross off a majority of their list, but miss the most important items!

▪ **No daily plan.** Beginning your day without a plan of action is a formula for spending all day doing the wrong things. It invites anyone and everyone to interrupt your activities. You will passively allow unwelcome intrusions, because you'll have no way to defend yourself. And you'll inevitably forget something important.

▪ **Perfectionism.** Are you unable to complete and release an assignment (paper, lab report, presentation, whatever) until it is done "perfectly"? Do you inevitably spend hours searching for ways to make every project better? Even if you can't find anything to improve, are you convinced there must be something you overlooked?

■ **Personal disorganization.** No matter how organized your priorities or how effective your daily plan, you may be losing irretrievable time searching for things that are lost in the messes on your desk, in your files, closets, and car.

■ **Interruptions.** Your day can be going according to schedule...until a friend drops in or a game of "Killer Frisbee" commences. Many of these occurrences can be eliminated; those that can't must be controlled... or at least worked into your schedule based on your priorities.

■ **Procrastination.** It always seems like a good idea to find something important to do around the house when a test looms. After all, as Scarlett O'Hara proclaimed, tomorrow is another day. Habitually failing to tackle important assignments will soon make your good grades "gone with the wind."

If some or all of these productivity problems apply to you, it's time to change some habits. If you're resolved to do so, you'll be encouraged to know that bad habits can be replaced by good ones relatively easily. In fact, it's easier to replace a habit than to break it. Here's your battle plan:

■ **Begin today.** The best time to start working on your resolve to be better organized is today. Don't procrastinate.

■ **Spread the word.** Don't keep your resolve a secret. Commit yourself to positive change by telling your friends and family what you've decided to do and by challenging them to hold you to your commitment.

■ **Practice, practice, practice.** Practice is the motor oil that lubricates any habit's engine. The more you do something, the more ingrained it becomes.

The Goal Pyramid

One way to visualize all your goals—and their relation to each other—is to construct what I call a goal pyramid. Here's how to do it:

1. Centered at the top of a piece of paper, write down what you hope to ultimately gain from your education. This is your long-range goal and the pinnacle of your pyramid.

2. Below your long-range goal(s), list mid-range goals— milestones or steps that will lead you to your eventual target.

3. Below the mid-range goals, list as many short-range goals as you can—smaller steps that can be completed in relatively short periods of time.

Change your goal pyramid as you progress through school. You may eventually decide on a different career. Or your mid-range goals may change as you decide on a different path leading to the long-range goal. The short-range goals will undoubtedly change, even daily.

The process of creating your own goal pyramid allows you to see how all those little daily and weekly steps you take can lead to your mid-range and long-term goals, and will thereby motivate you to work on your daily and weekly tasks with more energy and enthusiasm.

Make Goal Setting a Part of Your Life

The development of good study skills is the highway to your goals, whatever they are. No matter how hard you have to work or how much adversity you have to overcome along the way, the journey will indeed be worth it.

How do you make setting goals a part of your life? Here are some hints I think will help:

1. **Be realistic when you set goals.** Don't aim too high or too low, and don't be particularly concerned when (not if) you have to make adjustments along the way.

2. **Be realistic about your expectations.** An improved understanding of a subject you have little aptitude for is preferable to getting hopelessly bogged down if total mastery of the subject is just not in the cards.

3. **Don't give up too easily.** You can be overly realistic— too ready to give up just because something is a trifle harder than you'd like. Don't aim too high and feel miserable when you don't come close, or aim too low and never achieve your potential— find the path that's right for you.

4. **Concentrate on areas that offer the best chance for improvement.** Unexpected successes can do wonders for your confidence and might make it possible for you to achieve more than you thought you could, even in other areas.

5. **Monitor your achievements and keep resetting your goals.** Daily, weekly, monthly, yearly—ask yourself how you've done and where you'd like to go now.

6. **Put your goal pyramid right up on the wall.** See it. Feel it. Live it.

How Perfect Are You?

What is a perfectionist, and are you one? And if you are, why is it a problem? (If you answered no to the first two questions, you can freely skip this section. I suspect I'm speaking to a minority of my readers here.)

Perfectionists care perhaps too much, finding it impossible to be satisfied with anything less than "perfect" work (as they define it), presuming that such an ideal can actually be attained.

It is possible, of course, to score a "perfect" 100 on a test or to get an A+ on a paper the teacher calls "Perfect!" in the margin. But in reality, doing anything "perfectly" is an impossible task.

What does all this have to do with you? Nothing, unless you find yourself spending two hours polishing what is an already A+ paper or half an hour searching for that one "perfect" word or an hour rewriting great notes to make them "absolutely perfect." In other words, while striving for perfection may well be a noble trait, it can easily become an uncontrollable and unstoppable urge that seriously inhibits your enjoyment of your work and your life.

If you find yourself fighting this demon, remind yourself (frequently) of the Law of Diminishing Returns: Your initial effort yields the biggest results, with each succeeding effort yielding proportionately less. And there comes a point when even the most prodigious efforts yield negligible results. This applies not only to perfectionists, but also to those of you who scoff at the very thought of using a "simple" outline or producing a "formulaic" report.

You do not have to always be innovative, dazzling, and creative. You do not have to invent a "new, multimedia, interactive" book report. Sometimes a good six-page book report that gets an A– is just fine, and that A+ "innovation" is more trouble (and time) than it's worth!

When I am tempted to do far more than necessary, just because it would be a "cool" solution (and time consuming and wasteful and inefficient and difficult), I think of Georges Simenon, the French author best known for his Inspector Maigret mystery series...and the 500 total books he wrote in his lifetime. How did he do it and still have time to eat and sleep? Simple—he used only 2,000 vocabulary words (out of the 800,000 plus available to him) so he wouldn't have to interrupt his writing to consult a dictionary or thesaurus. (And he probably didn't eat or sleep much.)

If you really would prefer spending another couple of hours on that A+ paper or searching for a website your teacher has never heard of to taking in a movie, reading a book, or getting some other assignment done, be my guest. Is the last 10 percent or so really worth it? In some cases it is, but not usually.

Three More Concepts to Help You Get Organized

As you begin to make goal setting and organization a part of your daily life, here are three concepts that will make a huge difference in your success.

Small Changes, Over Time, Make a Big Difference

A simple, tiny change in your behavior may have virtually negligible results, but make hundreds of small changes, and the effects can be earth-shattering!

Make this rule become an automatic part of your thought process and your actions. It will help you understand the often small difference between success and failure, productivity and frustration, happiness and agony. It's so simple, it's deceptive. What is the key to your success? Maybe just a little more training. Maybe a slightly better method of planning. Maybe just one tiny bad habit overcome. Maybe all of these and more. Each one alone is almost inconsequential, but when added up, the advantage is incredible!

The 80–20 Rule (The Pareto Principle)

Another rule that you can apply to make a difference in how well you organize and manage your priorities is the 80–20 Rule, also known as the Pareto Principle.

Victor Pareto was an Italian economist and sociologist at the turn of the 20th century who studied the ownership of land in Italy. Pareto discovered that more than 80 percent of all the land was owned by less than 20 percent of the people.

As he studied other things that people owned (including money), he found the same principle held true: 20 percent or less of the people always ended up with 80 percent or more of whatever he measured.

The most astonishing revelation about the 80–20 Rule is its opposite side: If 20 percent of activities are producing 80 percent of the results, then the other 80 percent of activities are, in total, only giving 20 percent of the results.

Remember: To apply the 80–20 Rule to managing your priorities, remind yourself that 20 percent of the activities on your list are going to produce 80 percent of the results and payoff. Your question must constantly be, "Which activities are the 20-percenters?"

But don't get too hung up on statistics, especially misleading ones. An ex-partner of mine once noticed that 45 percent of the books published one year made most of the profits, so he instructed everyone to just publish the 45 percent next year that would make money. Think about it.

Take Advantage of "In-between" Time

You can be even more productive if you identify and take advantage of the little windows of opportunity that pass through your life each day. They don't arrive with much fanfare, so if you're not alert to them, they will sneak right past you. What must you do with this "in-between" time, while you're stuck in traffic, waiting in line, or sitting by the phone? Recognize it as soon as it occurs and utilize it immediately by taking a premeditated action. If you don't have a plan, you will waste this time!

Here are some suggestions:

- Make phone calls.
- Read something.
- Mail letters.
- Pick up groceries (or make your grocery list).
- Clean up your desk and return things to their proper places.
- Review your daily schedule and reprioritize, if necessary.
- Go through your mail.
- Write a quick note or email.
- Proofread some or all of one of your papers.
- Think! (Take a few moments to think about an upcoming assignment, a paper you're writing, etc.)
- Relax!

CHAPTER 3

ORGANIZE YOUR STUDIES

You can study smarter. You can put in less time and get better results. But learning how to do so is hard, because learning of any kind takes discipline. And self-discipline is, for many of us, the most difficult task of all.

If you're currently doing little or nothing in the way of school-work, then you are going to have to put in more time and effort. How much more?

The smarter you are and the more easily you learn and adapt the techniques in this book, the more likely you'll be spending less time on your homework than before. But the further you need to go—from Ds to As rather than Bs to As—the more you need to learn and the longer you need to give yourself to learn it.

Don't get discouraged. You will see results surprisingly quickly.

Get Ready for a Lifelong Journey

Learning how to study is really a long-term process. Once you undertake the journey, you will be surprised at the number of landmarks, pathways, side streets, and road signs you'll find. Even after you've transformed yourself into a better student than you'd ever hoped to be, you'll inevitably find one more signpost that offers new information, one more pathway that leads you in an interesting new direction.

Consider learning how to study a lifelong process, and be ready to modify anything you're doing as you learn other methods.

This is especially important right from the start, when you consider your overall study strategies. How long should you study per night? How do you allocate time between subjects? How often should you schedule breaks? Your answers to these questions are going to vary considerably depending on how well you were doing before you read this book, how far you have to go, how interested you are in getting there, how involved you are in other activities, the time of day, your general health, and a host of other individual facts. Are you getting the idea?

It gets more complicated: What's your study sequence? Hardest assignments first? Easiest? Longest? Shortest? Are you comfortable switching back and forth from one to another, or do you prefer to focus on a single assignment from start to finish?

This gets even more difficult when you consider that the tasks themselves may have a great effect on your schedule. Fifteen-minute study unit increments might work well for you most of the time. I suspect half an hour is an ideal unit for most of you. And some of you will have no trouble working for an hour straight or even longer without a break.

On the other hand, you may find it easy to work on a long project in fits and starts, 15 or 20 minutes at a time, without needing to retrace your steps each time you pick it up again.

What's the lesson in all of this? There is no ideal, no answer—certainly no "right" answer—to many of the questions I've posed. It's a message you'll read in these pages over and over again: Figure out what works for you and keep on doing it. If it later stops working or doesn't seem to be working as well, change it.

None of the organizational techniques discussed at length in this book is carved in stone. Not only should you feel free to adapt and shape and bend them to your own needs, you must do so.

Creating Your Study Environment

On page 32 I have included a checklist for you to rate your study environment. It includes not just where you study—at home, in the library, at a friend's place—but when and how you study, too. Once you've identified what works for you, avoid those situations in which you know you don't perform best. If you don't know the answer to one or more of the questions, take the time to experiment.

My Ideal Study Environment

How I receive information best:

1. ❏ Orally   ❏ Visually

In the classroom, I should:

2. ❏ Concentrate on taking notes
   ❏ Concentrate on listening
3. ❏ Sit up front   ❏ Sit in back
   ❏ Sit near a window or door

Where I study best:

4. ❏ At home   ❏ In the library
   ❏ Somewhere else: _____

When I study best:

5. ❏ Every night; a little on weekends
   ❏ Mainly on weekends
   ❏ Spread out over seven days
6. ❏ In the morning   ❏ Evening   ❏ Afternoon
7. ❏ Before dinner   ❏ After dinner

How I study best:

8. ❏ Alone   ❏ With a friend   ❏ In a group
9. ❏ Under time pressure   ❏ Before I know I have to
10. ❏ With music   ❏ In front of the TV
    ❏ In a quiet room
11. ❏ Organizing an entire night's studying before I start
    ❏ Tackling and completing one subject at a time

I need to take a break:

12. ❏ Every 30 minutes or so   ❏ Every hour
    ❏ Every 2 hours   ❏ Every ____ hours

Study Groups

I was 35 years old and a devoted watcher of the television show *The Paper Chase* before I was introduced to the concept of a study group. This series was supposed to be about a law school that seemed just this side of hell, so sharing the load with other students wasn't just a good idea—it was virtually mandatory. My high school wasn't hell—not even a mild purgatory—but I still think a study group would have been beneficial. If I had thought of the idea, I probably would have started one.

The concept is simple: Find a small group of like-minded students and share notes, question each other, and prepare for tests together. To be effective, obviously, the students you pick for your group should share all, or at least most, of your classes.

Even if you find only one or two other students willing to work with you, such cooperation will be invaluable, especially in preparing for major exams.

Tips for Forming Your Own Study Group

- I suggest four students minimum, probably six maximum. You want to ensure everyone gets a chance to participate while maximizing the collective knowledge and wisdom of the group.

- While group members needn't be best friends, they shouldn't be overtly hostile to one another, either. Seek diversity of experience and demand common dedication.

- Try to select students who are at least as smart, committed, and serious as you. That will encourage you to keep up and challenge you a bit. Avoid a group in which you're the "star"—at least until you flicker out during the first exam.

- Avoid inviting members who are inherently unequal—boyfriend/girlfriend combinations, in which one may be inhibited by the other's presence; situations where one student works for another; situations where underclassmen and upperclassmen may stifle one another, etc.

- Decide early on if you're forming a study group or a social group. If the latter, don't pretend it's the former. If the former, don't just invite your friends and sit around discussing your teachers.

- There are a number of ways to organize. My suggestion is to assign each class to one student. That student must master that assigned class, completing any supplemental assigned reading, taking outstanding notes, outlining the course (if the group so desires), being available for questions, and preparing various practice quizzes, midterms, and finals as needed.

Needless to say, all of the other students should still attend all classes, take their own notes, and do their own reading and homework assignments. But the student assigned that class should attempt to master it, to actually become the "substitute professor" of that class in the study group.

So if you have five classes, a five person study group is ideal.

■ Make meeting times and assignments formal and rigorous. Consider establishing rigid rules of conduct. Better to shake out the nonserious students early. You don't want anyone who is working as little as possible but hoping to take advantage of your hard work.

■ Consider appointing a chair (rotating weekly, if you wish) in charge of keeping everyone on schedule and settling disputes before they disrupt the study group.

However you organize, clearly decide—early—the specific responsibilities of each student. Again, you never want the feeling to emerge that one or two participants are trying to "ride the coattails" of the others.

Where Should You Study?

1. **At the library.** There may be numerous choices, from the large reading room to quieter, sometimes deserted, specialty rooms to your own solitary study cubicle. My favorite "home away from home" at Princeton was a little room that seemingly only four or five of us knew about— with wonderfully comfortable chairs, subdued lighting, phonographs with earplugs, and a selection of some 500 classical records. For someone like me, who required music to study, it was a custom-made study haven!

2. **At home.** Remember that this is the place where distractions are most likely to occur. No one tends to telephone you at the library, and little brothers (or your own kids) will not find you easily in the "stacks." It is, of course, usually the most convenient place to make your study headquarters. It may not, however, be the most effective.

3. At a friend's, neighbor's, or relative's house.
This may not be an option for most of you, even on
an occasional basis, but you still may want to set up
one or two alternative study sites. Despite the fact
that it's better if you can study in the same place every
night, I have a friend who needs variety to motivate
himself. So he has four study locations and simply
rotates them from night to night. Do whatever works
best for you.

4. In an empty classroom. Certainly an option at
many colleges and perhaps some private high schools,
it is an interesting idea mainly because so few students
have ever thought of it! While not a likely option at
a public high school, it never hurts to ask if you can
make some arrangement. Since many athletic teams
practice until 6 p.m. or later, even on the high school
level, there may be a part of the school open—and
usable with permission—even if the rest is locked
up tight.

5. At your job. Whether you're a student working
part-time or a full-time worker going to school part-
time, you may be able to make arrangements to use
an empty office, even during regular office hours, or
perhaps after everyone has left (depending on how
much your boss trusts you). If you're in junior high or
high school and a parent, friend, or relative works
nearby, you may be able to work from just after
school until closing time at that person's workplace.

Whatever place you choose for your study area, make it one place if at all possible, a single location that is only for study, which leaves out your bed, in front of the TV, and the dining room table, among other bad choices.

Just as you (hopefully) sit right down and go to work when you enter a classroom (presuming the teacher is in the room!), your attitude and attention will be automatic if you associate your study area solely with homework, not sleeping, eating, or entertaining yourself. And that will make the time you spend more effective and efficient.

When Should You Study?

As much as possible, create a routine time of day for your studying. Some experts contend that doing the same thing at the same time every day is the most effective way to organize any ongoing task. Some students find it easier to set aside specific blocks of time during the day, each day, in which they plan on studying.

No matter who you are, the time of day you'll study is determined by these factors:

1. **Study when you're at your best.** What is your peak performance period—the time of day you do your best work? This period varies from person to person— you may be dead to the world until noon but able to study well into the night, or up and alert at the crack of dawn but distracted and tired if you try to burn the midnight oil. Just remember, focus = efficiency.

2. **Consider your sleep habits.** Habit is a very powerful influence. If you always set your alarm for 7 a.m., you may soon start waking up just before the alarm goes off. If you have grown accustomed to going to sleep around 11 p.m., you will undoubtedly become quite tired if you try to study until 2 a.m., and probably accomplish very little in those three extra hours.

3. **Study when you can.** Although you want to sit down to study when you are mentally most alert, external factors also play a role in deciding when you study. Being at your best is a great goal, but is not always possible. Study whenever circumstances allow.

4. **Consider the complexity of the assignment when you allocate time.** The tasks themselves may have a great effect on your schedule. Don't schedule 1 hour for an 80-page reading assignment when you know you read half a page per minute...on a good day.

5. **Use "nonprime" hours for the easiest tasks.** When your energy and motivation are at their lowest levels, should you really bore in on that project that's been giving you fits? Or merely recopy some notes, go over your calendar, or proofread a paper? When you're least creative, least energetic, and least motivated, why would you even consider tackling your most challenging assignments? Don't be like many businesspeople I know who schedule their time backwards: In the morning, when they're raring to go, they read the paper, check their email, and skim trade journals. At the end of the day, when they can barely see straight, they start on the presentation for the Board of Directors' meeting...tomorrow's Board of Directors' meeting.

6. Schedule study time immediately after class or, if that's not possible, immediately before. This is most pertinent for college and graduate students, who can usually schedule their own class time and may have significant free time between classes. Your memory of a class is, not surprisingly, strongest immediately after it, so allocating an open hour after class to go over notes, think about the lecture, and complete that day's assignment is the best way to spend that hour.

If that isn't possible, then taking the time to study immediately before class is an excellent second option, especially if you usually need that time to complete your assignments!

Evaluate Your Study Area

Whatever location you choose as your study base, how you set up your study area can affect your ability to stay focused and, if you aren't careful, seriously inhibit quality study time. Sit down at your desk or study area right now and evaluate your own study environment:

1. Do you have one or two special places reserved just for studying? Or do you study wherever seems convenient or available at the time?

2. Is your study area a pleasant place? Would you tout it to a friend as a good place to study? Or do you dread it because it's so depressing?

3. How's the lighting? Is it too dim or too bright? Is the entire desk area well lit?

4. Are all the materials you need handy?

5. What else do you do here? Do you eat? Sleep? Play computer games? Read for pleasure? If you try to study at the same place you sit to listen to music or chat on the phone, you may find yourself doing one when you think you're doing the other!

6. Is your study area in a high-traffic area? How often are you interrupted by people passing through?

7. Can you close the door to the room to avoid disturbances and outside noise?

8. When do you spend the most time here? What time of day do you study? Is it when you are at your best? Or do you inevitably study when you're tired and less productive?

9. Are your files, folders, and other class materials organized and near the work area? Do you have an effective filing system in place for them?

10. Set up a "future" drawer in your filing cabinet. When you find ideas, research material, etc. (from magazines, books, newspapers, websites, whatever) that you think may be important sometime in the future, write a pertinent note to yourself and file it. The time you take now will be a mere fraction of the time you save in the future.

Staying Focused on Your Studies

If you find yourself doodling and dawdling more than reading and remembering, try these solutions:

1. **Create a work environment in which you're comfortable.** The size, style, and placement of your desk, chair, and lighting may all affect whether or not you're distracted from the work at hand. Take the time to design the area that's perfect for you.

2. **Turn up the lights.** Experiment with the placement and intensity of lighting in your study area until you find what works for you, both in terms of comfort and as a means of staying awake and focused.

3. **Set some rules.** Let family, relatives, and especially friends know how important your studying is and that specific hours are inviolate.

4. **Take the breaks you need.** Don't blindly follow well-intentioned but bogus advice about how long you should study before taking a break. Break when you need to. But don't let your break time exceed your study time!

Fighting Tiredness and Boredom

You've chosen the best study spot, and no one could fault you on its setup. So why are you still using pencils to prop up your eyelids? Here's what to do if your energy has taken a brief vacation.

Take a nap. What a concept! When you're too tired to study, take a short nap to revive yourself. Maximize that nap's effect by keeping it short—20 minutes is ideal, 40 minutes absolute maximum. After that, you go into another phase of sleep and you may wake even more tired than before.

Have a drink. A little caffeine won't harm you—a cup of coffee or tea, a glass of soda. Just be careful not to mainline it—caffeine's "wake-up" properties seem to reverse when you reach a certain level, making you far more tired than you were!

Turn down the heat. You needn't build an igloo out back, but too warm a room will inevitably leave you dreaming of sugarplums...while your paper remains unwritten on your desk.

Shake a leg. Go for a walk, high step around the kitchen, do a few jumping jacks—even mild physical exertion will give you an immediate lift.

Change your study schedule. Presuming you have some choice here, find a way to study when you are normally more awake and/or most efficient.

Studying with Small Kids

Since so many more people are going to school while raising a family, I want to give you some ideas that will help you cope with the Charge of the Preschool Light Brigade.

Plan activities to keep the kids occupied. The busier you are in school and/or at work, the more time your kids will want to spend with you when you are home. If you spend some time with them, it may be easier for them to play alone, especially if you've created projects they can work on while you're working on your homework.

Make the kids part of your study routine. Kids love routine, so why not include them in yours? If 4 p.m. to 6 p.m. is always "Mommy's Study Time," they will soon get used to it, especially if you make spending other time with them a priority and give them something creative and fun to do during those hours.

Use the television as a babysitter. While many of you will have a problem with this—it's one that my daughter and I dealt with weekly, if not daily—it may be the lesser of two evils. And you can certainly rent (or DVR) enough quality shows so you don't have to worry about the little darlings watching movies about street gangs bashing skulls (or bashing skulls themselves on some video game system).

Plan your study accordingly. Unless you are right up there in the Perfect Parent Pantheon, all these things will not keep your kids from interrupting every now and then. While you can minimize such intrusions, it's virtually impossible to eliminate them entirely. So don't try—plan your schedule assuming them. For one, that means taking more frequent breaks to spend five minutes with your kids. They'll be more likely to give you the 15 or 20 minutes at a time you need if they get periodic attention themselves.

Find help. Spouses can occasionally take the kids out for dinner and a movie. (And trust me, the kids will encourage you to study more if you institute this practice!) Relatives can babysit (at their homes) on a rotating basis. Playmates can be invited over (allowing you to send your darling to their house the next day). You may be able to trade child care responsibilities and play dates with other parents at school. And professional day care may be available at your child's school or in someone's home for a couple of hours a day.

CHAPTER 4

ORGANIZE YOUR CALENDAR

N ow you're ready to plan!

We'll begin by developing a time-management plan for an entire term...before it begins, of course. This will allow you to keep your sights on the "big picture." You'll see the forest, even when you're in the midst of the trees...and they're oversized redwoods.

By being able to take in your entire term—every major assignment, every test, every paper, every appointment—you will be less likely to get caught up spending too much time on a lower priority assignment while falling behind on a more important one.

And when you can actually see you have a test in accounting the same week your zoology project is due, you can plan ahead and finish the project early. If you decide (for whatever reason) not to do so, at least you won't be caught by surprise when crunch time comes.

Start Planning Early

For your long-term planning to be effective, however, you must start early. If you fail to plan before the school term begins, you will probably find yourself wasting time filling in your schedule one event at a time during the term. You may also find yourself feeling disorganized throughout the term. Starting early, on the other hand, increases your ability to follow a systematic plan of attack.

All college students—and some high school students—are able to pick and choose courses according to their own schedules, likes, dislikes, goals, etc. The giddiness of such freedom should be tempered with the commonsense approach you're trying to develop by reading this book. Here are a few hints to help you along:

1. Whenever possible, consider each professor's reputation as you decide whether to select a particular course, especially if it is an overview or introductory course offered in two or three sessions. Word soon gets around as to which professors' lectures are stimulating and rewarding—an environment in which learning is a joy, even if it isn't a subject you like!

2. If there's a course you think you'd like to take but suspect or know you can't fit it in this semester (or even this year), take the time now to check out course requirements, assignments, reading list, etc., and go to the first class. This is generally an overview of the entire course and the time when most professors hand out syllabuses, long-term assignments, and suggested reading lists. You may not be sure you want to take the course before that class, but you'll certainly have a better idea afterwards.

3. Attempt to select classes that balance your schedule on a weekly and even a daily basis, though this will not always be possible or advisable. (Don't change your major just to fit your schedule!) Try to leave an open hour or half-hour between classes—it's ideal for review, post-class note taking, quick trips to the library, etc.

4. Try to alternate challenging classes with those that come more easily to you. Studying is a process of positive reinforcement. You'll need encouragement along the way.

5. Avoid late evening or early morning classes, especially if such scheduling provides you with large gaps of "down time." And if you're not a "morning person," don't even think of taking a class that meets daily at 8:00 a.m. I did it my freshman year of college and managed to attend, oh, at least three times.

6. Set a personal study pace and follow it. Place yourself on a study diet, the key rule of which is: Don't overeat.

Identify the Starting Line

You can't race off to your ultimate goal until you figure out where your starting line is. So the first step necessary to overhaul your current routine is to identify that routine in detail. There are two ways to go about this, and I suggest you do both.

The first is to use the chart on page 48 to assess how much time you actually have available for studying. If it's clearly not enough, then you'd better reassess how much time you're spending in each of the other areas. You may have to cut your part-time work hours, quit a club, even change your schedule to reduce your commute. Of course, if you're spending two hours a day on "grooming" or six hours eating, the solution may be a little more obvious.

Where Does Your Time Go?

	Hrs./Day	Days/Wk	Hrs./Wk
Meals (including prep and cleanup)	_____	7	_____
Sleeping (including naps)	_____	7	_____
Grooming	_____	7	_____
Commuting	_____	5?	_____
Errands	_____	7	_____
Extracurricular activities	_____	_____	_____
Part- or full-time job	_____	_____	_____
In class	_____	_____	_____
Entertainment*	_____	_____	_____

*Hanging with friends, going out, watching TV, reading for pleasure, etc.

Fill in the first column, multiply by the second, then total the third column. There are 168 hours in a week (24 × 7). How many do you currently have left for studying? Note: Any answer that contains a minus is a *bad* sign.

You should create a second chart yourself. Write down, in 15-minute increments, how you spend your time right now. While keeping track of your activities for a day or two might be sufficient for some of you, I recommend you chart them for an entire week, including the weekend.

This is especially important if, like many people, you have huge pockets of time that seemingly disappear, but in reality are devoted to things like "resting" after you wake up, putting on makeup or shaving, reading the paper, waiting for transportation, or driving to and from school or work. Could you use an extra hour or two a day, either for studying or for fun? Make better use of such "dead" time and you'll find all the time you need.

Learn how to do multiple tasks at the same time: Listen to a book on tape while you're working around the house; practice vocabulary or math drills while you're driving; or have your kids, parents, or roommates quiz you for an upcoming test while you are doing the dishes, vacuuming, or dusting. And always carry your calendar, notebook(s), pens, and a textbook with you—you can get a phenomenal amount of reading or studying done while in line at the bank, in the library, the supermarket, or on a bus or train.

Identify those items on your daily calendar, whatever their priority, that can be completed in 15 minutes or less. These are the ideal tasks to tackle during that "dead" time.

Collect What You Need

As you begin your planning session, make sure you have all the information and materials you need to make a quality plan. Gather your class syllabuses; work schedule; dates of important family events, vacations or trips, other personal commitments (doctor appointments, birthday parties, etc.); and a calendar of any extracurricular events in which you plan to participate.

There are only two items you need to become the most organized person you know: a long-term planning calendar that can be tacked onto a wall and a daily calendar you can carry with you.

Keeping track of your day-to-day activities—classes, appointments, regular daily homework assignments, and daily or weekly quizzes—will be dealt with later in this chapter. For now, I want to talk about the projects—term papers, theses, studying for midterm and final exams, etc.—that require completion over a long period of time— weeks, maybe even months.

Your Long-Term Planning Calendar

It's not necessary for you to construct your own calendar, though it's certainly the least expensive alternative. There are ready-made wall and desk calendars available in a variety of formats for your convenience, including magnetic and erasable. Your local office supply, stationery, or bookstore will have a selection of them. I suggest at least a three-month calendar. You could certainly use a six-month or even a yearly calendar.

You will not be filling this calendar with a great deal of detail, so the spaces in which you will write do not have to be humongous. This calendar is the overview of your schedule, a kind of "life-at-a-glance" summary of those items and appointments occurring more than one week in the future. (If they are happening this week, they will be in your daily calendar, but I'm ahead of myself.)

So start by entering the date for every major test, when papers and projects are due, future appointments (yes, this isn't just for schoolwork), and anything else that you must remember. I have reproduced a single month from a typical calendar on page 60. Notice that there is little detail. It's a snapshot, remember?

Your Daily Calendar

This is the most essential tool you can utilize, and one you absolutely must. Find a format that works for you. I prefer one like that reproduced on pages 62–63, with Monday, Tuesday, and Wednesday on a left-hand sheet and Thursday through Sunday on a right. Whether in a notebook or spiral-bound, this format gives you the entire week at a glance and more than enough room to write in great detail. I find that reason enough to avoid electronic PDAs and those appointment books that give you one day per page. You may get a lot more room to write, but you'll find yourself doing a lot of flipping around just to see what's happening tomorrow or the next day.

In the filled-in sample calendar on pages 62–63, our student—let's call her Lindsay—did a pretty good job. She didn't just jot down homework assignments. First, she prioritized them— those As, Bs, and Cs to the left of each entry.

Next, she estimated the amount of time each would take (in the "T" for "Time" column) and how long it actually took (in the "A" for "Actual" column). She used minutes, but you certainly can use fractions of an hour if you find it easier. Whatever total time you wind up allocating should, obviously, approximate the time you have available to study. If you find yourself habitually spending more time on each assignment than you have projected, consider adding a "safety margin" to your estimates. Then total all the estimates and make sure you haven't scheduled yourself till 4:00 a.m.!

Finally, Lindsay included more than just homework assignments—she jotted reminders to herself about grocery shopping, phone calls she had to make, band practice, and a host of other things.

There are also assigned projects that are not due this week— an English paper, an upcoming quiz in geometry, a bigger test in history. Lindsay scheduled time to choose a topic for her English paper, get the teacher's approval, and even begin preliminary research. She also planned time to study for both geometry and history.

The dates when future projects are due and future tests scheduled actually are recorded twice—once in her daily calendar and again in her long-term calendar. But the steps necessary to write her paper and the time she needs to allocate for studying are only on her daily calendar. (This is not a hard-and-fast rule. You can certainly include steps necessary for future projects on your long-term planning calendar, too. I prefer not to muddle it up with too much detail.)

What else should you notice about Lindsay's daily calendar? She has done a good job prioritizing—assignments due the next day are "A" priorities, and those due later are "B" or even "C" priorities. She has dutifully projected the time she will spend on each assignment and recorded how long each actually took. And she saved herself the time of looking up phone numbers by recording them right in her calendar.

Unfortunately, Lindsay isn't doing the greatest job projecting how long her homework will actually take her. Geometry always takes her longer than she thinks it will, and her biology lab report clearly was more complicated than she expected. She's taken the time to schedule five total hours for band rehearsal…but spent eight, which is probably why she failed to do any preliminary research for her English paper. And it's not clear whether she's scheduled "make-up time" during the next week.

If you set up and use your daily calendar this way, you will quickly discover it is your life. You will always carry it with you, and you will die a horrible death if you ever misplace it or, heaven forbid, lose it.

Leave your long-term planning calendar on your wall or desk at home, and carry your daily calendar with you—everywhere. Whenever new projects, appointments, meetings, etc., are scheduled, add them immediately to your daily calendar. Then transfer key dates to your long-term planning calendar.

Remember: If it's a simple task and will definitely be accomplished within a week—read pages 201 through 274, study for quiz, proofread a paper—it belongs in your daily calendar.

If, however, it's a task that is complicated—requiring further breakdown into specific steps—and/or one that will require more than a week to complete—the final due date should be entered on your long-term calendar, then the individual steps added to your daily calendar.

And if a major test is coming up, I've included a special Pretest Organizer at the end of this chapter. You'll never have to worry again about not having the materials you need when you're ready to study.

The Fat Lady Isn't Singing Yet

For any time-management system to work, it has to be used continually. Before you go on, make an appointment with yourself for the end of the week—Sunday night is perfect— to sit down and plan for the following week. You don't have to spend a lot of time—half an hour is probably all it will take to review your commitments for the week and schedule the necessary study time.

Despite its brevity, this may just be the best time you spend all week, because you will reap the benefits of it throughout the week and beyond!

First, identify anything you need to do this week that is not yet written on your daily calendar. Look at your long-term calendar to determine what tasks need to be completed this week for all of your major school projects. Add any additional tasks that must be done—from sending a birthday present to your sister to attending your monthly volunteer meeting to completing homework that may have just been assigned.

Remember to break any long-term or difficult projects into small, "bite-size" tasks that can be included on your schedule. As Henry Ford said, "Nothing is particularly hard if you divide it into small jobs." Hence, the assembly line.

Once you have created your list, you can move on to the next step—putting your tasks in order of importance.

Prioritize Your Tasks

When you sit down to study without a plan, you just dive into the first project that comes to mind. The problem with this approach has been discussed earlier: There is little guarantee that the first thing that comes to mind is the most important.

If you find yourself forgetting to transfer data back and forth from your long-term calendar to your daily calendar (or vice versa), or you simply need even more help keeping the most important tasks in mind, a Priority Task Sheet is another tool you can use. Its sole purpose is to help you arrange your tasks in order of importance (not to record them—that's the job of your calendar). That way, even if you find yourself without enough time for everything, you can at least finish the most important assignments. You can't effectively deal with today's priorities if you still have to contend with yesterday's...or last week's!

First, ask yourself this question: "If I only got a few things done this week, what would I want them to be?" Mark these high-priority tasks with an "H" or an "A." After you have identified the "urgent" items, consider those tasks that are least important—items that could wait until the following week to be done, if necessary. (This may include tasks you consider very important but that don't have to be completed this week.) These are low-priority items, at least for this week—mark them with an "L" or a "C."

All the other items fit somewhere between the critical tasks and the low-priority ones. Review the remaining items. If you're sure none of them are particularly low or high priority, mark them with an "M," for middle priority, or a "B."

If you push aside the same low-priority item day after day, week after week, at some point you should just stop and decide whether it's something you need to do at all! This is a strategic way to make a task or problem "disappear." In the business world, some managers purposefully avoid confronting a number of problems, waiting to see if they will simply solve themselves through benign neglect. If it works in business, it can work in school. (But if you find yourself consistently moving "B" or even "A" priorities from day to day, reassess your system. Something's broken.)

A completed Priority Task Sheet is on page 61. A blank Priority Task Sheet you can photocopy is on page 64.

Have you been taking the time to estimate how long each task will take, and adjusting your projections when it's clear certain tasks invariably take longer than you think? Terrific! Here's a way to use such estimating as a great motivator: Instead of writing down how long a task will take, write down the time within which you intend to finish it. What's the difference? It has now become a goal. It may put just the slightest amount of pressure on you, making you try just a little harder to finish on time.

You can take this goal-setting technique further. Write down the times you expect to finish each page of a 10-page reading assignment, or each one of the 20 math problems you have to complete. Setting such small time goals is a great motivator and a fantastic way to maximize your concentration and minimize daydreaming.

If You Run Out of Time to Eat or Sleep

You may be doing a good job staying on top of school assignments and other priorities, but a lousy job actually living your life. If so, you can consider making your calendar even more detailed by filling in the "givens"—the time you need to sleep, eat, work, and attend class—before you start adding papers, projects, homework, study time, etc., to your calendar.

Even if your current routine consists of meals on the run and sleep whenever you find it, build the assumption right into your schedule that you are going to get eight hours of sleep and three decent meals a day. You may surprise yourself and find that there is still enough time to do everything you need. (Though all of us probably know someone who sleeps three hours a night, eats nothing but junk, and still finds a way to get straight As, most experts would contend that regular, healthy eating and a decent sleep schedule are key attributes to any successful study system.)

Just be careful. It is very easy to get so enthralled with how organized you are that you begin to "over-schedule" your life. It's the easiest way to get overwhelmed and the most common reason students quit using a basic time-management system.

Other Considerations

In addition to the importance of the task and the available time you have to complete it, other factors will determine how you fit everything you have to do into the time available. Some factors will be beyond your control—your work schedule, appointments with professors, counselors, or doctors. But there are plenty of factors you do control and should consider as you put together your calendar each week.

Schedule enough time for each task—time to "warm up" and get the task accomplished, but, particularly when working on long-term projects, not so much time that you "burn out."

Every individual is different, but most students study best in blocks of 30–45 minutes, depending on the subject.

Don't overdo it. Plan your study time in blocks, breaking up work time with short leisure activities. (It's helpful to add these to your schedule as well.) For example, you've set aside three hours on Wednesday afternoon for that research assignment. Schedule a 15-minute walk to the ice cream shop somewhere in the middle of that study block. You'll find that these breaks help you think more clearly and creatively when you get back to studying.

Even if you tend to like longer blocks of study time, be careful about scheduling study "marathons"—a six- or eight-hour stretch rather than a series of one- or two-hour sessions. The longer the period you schedule, the more likely you'll have to fight the demons of procrastination and daydreaming. Convincing yourself that you are really studying your heart out, you'll also find it easier to justify time-wasting distractions, scheduling longer breaks and, before long, quitting before you should.

Finally, remember Parkinson's Law: "Work expands so as to fill the time available for its completion." In other words, if you fail to schedule a one-hour block for a project that should take an hour, you will probably be surprised to find (eureka!) that it somehow takes two or three!

Use These Tools Daily

Each night (or during breakfast), look at your schedule for the upcoming day. How much free time is there? Are there "surprise" tasks that are not on your schedule but need to be? Are there conflicts you were unaware of at the beginning of the week?

If you plan well at the beginning of the week, this shouldn't happen often. But it invariably does. Just as often, you'll discover a class is canceled or a meeting postponed, which leaves you with a schedule change. By checking your calendar daily—either the night before or the first thing in the morning—you'll be able to respond to these changes.

I like to plan everything out just before I "shut down" for the night. It's a fantastic feeling to wake up and start the day completely organized!

The Most Important 15 Minutes of Your Day

Set aside 15 minutes every day to go over your daily and weekly priorities. While many businesspeople like to make this the first 15 minutes of their day, I recommend making it the last 15 minutes of your day. Why? Three great reasons:

1. **Your ideas will be fresher.** It's easier to analyze at the end of the day what you've accomplished...and haven't.

2. **It's a great way to end the day.** Even if your "study day" ends at 11 p.m., you'll feel fully prepared for the next day and ready to relax, anxiety-free.

3. **You'll get off to a great start the next morning.** If you use the morning to plan, it's easy to turn a 15 minute planning session into an hour of aimless "thinking." While others are fumbling for a cup of coffee, you're off and running!

Long-term Calendar (Filled-in Sample)

MONTH: January

MON	TUE	WED	THU	FRI	SAT	SUN
1	2	3	4	5	6	7
	Gorbachev rough paper due			French vocab quiz	Mom visit →	→
8	9	10	11	12	13	14
	English midterm	Geometry midterm	History midterm			
15	16	17	18	19	20	21
					Lacrosse tourney →	→
22	23	24	25	26	27	28
		First 2 parts of French project due		French vocab quiz	Lacrosse tourney →	→
29	30	31				

Priority Task Sheet (Filled-in Sample)

Priority Rating	Schedule	Priority Tasks This Week
		Priority Tasks This Week Week of **3/28** through **4/3**
		Sociology paper
H		**Library search*
M		**Outline*
L		**Rough draft*
		Math assignments
H		**Chapter 4*
M		**Chapter 5*
M		**Study for test*

Daily Calendar (Filled-in Sample)

> *January*

20	Monday		T	A	Notes
A	Geometry	probs 24–42 odd	40	60	pick up milk & eggs
A	History	Read Chap 3	30	40	Don't forget homework!
A	Biology	Finish lab report	60	25	
	Read Chapter 8	30	25		
C	Choose English topic		20	15	
	Check with teacher		10	10	
A	Bring gym shorts tomorrow				
B	Call Cheryl right after sch.				
A	7PM Band rehearsal		120	180	

21	Tuesday		T	A	Notes
C	Health	Redo chart (due Fri)	30	20	
A	Geometry	24-42 Even	40	70	
B	Spanish	Essay rough draft	75	120	See Mr. Dawkins for
					Thursday Appt.
B	Band 6:30		120	150	

22	Wednesday		T	A	Notes
A	Spanish	Essay final draft	60	70	
	proof	30	30		
A	History	Chap 4	30	45	
B	Biology	Chap 9	30	45	
		probs p.112	50	30	

Daily Calendar (Filled-in Sample)

January

23	Thursday	T	A	Notes
A	Finalize Health chart, proof	20	40	
B	research English paper	120	0	2:30 Mr. Dawkins
	(online)			@ Lib. office
				Bring gym shorts!
				Dr. Gevens 5PM
	Band 6:30	60	150	

24	Friday	T	A	Notes
B	Geometry probs 85-110	50	90	
				Jerry - Are u picking me
				up tonight?
				What time?
				Bring PJs
Call:	Rob 742-6891			Toothbrush
	Jack 742-2222			Makeup
	Ira 743-8181			CDs (see list)
	Cheryl 777-7777			

25	Saturday	T	A	Notes
A	Study for Geometry quiz	120	90	
B	Study for Hist. midterm	120	120	
	(Feb 3)			
A	Biology probs pp. 113-114	60	45	

26	Sunday	T	A	Notes
	ENJOY!			
				Call mom!
	Church 11AM			
	Brunch @ Amy's 2PM			

Priority Task Sheet

Priority Rating	Schedule	Priority Tasks This Week
		Week of _____ through _____

Daily Calendar

		T	A	Notes

		T	A	Notes

		T	A	Notes

Pretest Organizer

Class: _____   **Teacher:** _____

Test date: _____   **Time:** From: _____   To: _____

Place: _____

Special instructions to myself (e.g., take calculator, dictionary, etc.):

Materials I need to study for this test (check all needed):

_____ Book   _____ DVDs/tapes/videos

_____ Workbook   _____ Old tests

_____ Class notes   _____ Other

_____ Handouts

Format of the test (write the number of T/F, essays, and so forth, and total points for each section):

_____

_____

_____

_____

_____

_____

Study group meetings (times, places):

1. _____

2. _____

3. _____

4. _____

5. _____

Material to be covered:

Indicate topics, sources, and amount of review (light or heavy) required. Check box when review is completed.

Topic	Sources	Review
_____	_____	_____
_____	_____	_____
_____	_____	_____
_____	_____	_____
_____	_____	_____
_____	_____	_____
_____	_____	_____

After the test:

Grade I expected _____   Grade I received _____

What did I do that helped me?

_____

_____

_____

_____

_____

What else should I have done?

_____

_____

_____

_____

_____

_____

CHAPTER 5

DEALING WITH
LIFE'S DAILY TRAUMAS

Your organizational plan should be simple, like the one I detailed in the previous chapter. Why commit to another complicated project that taxes your time and mental energies? Yet, no matter how basic and easy to use your program may be, there's no guarantee you won't be plagued with an occasional time crunch. Anticipate some glitches and develop the problem-solving skills you need to ensure that study roadblocks don't stop your progress completely.

If you run into a "wall" on your path to organizational success, the best solution is to find creative ways around it, rather than trying to crash your way through it.

Time Flies When You're Having Fun...

...and sometimes even when you're not. No matter how hard you try to stick to your schedule, you may find that your assignments always take longer than planned. You schedule an hour to do your economics homework, and it takes you twice that long. You plan an afternoon at the library for research, and it's closing time before you're ready to leave. It seems like you spend all your time studying—and you're still not getting everything done.

Solution: It's time for an attitude check. Are you being too much of a perfectionist? Is it taking you so long to read because you're trying to memorize every word? Make sure your expectations are realistic. And don't exaggerate the importance of lower priority assignments.

Consider altering your behavior—with a little help from an alarm clock. If you've planned an hour for your reading assignment, set the clock to go off when you should have completed it. Then, stop reading and go on to the next assignment. If you're not done, reassure yourself that you can go back to it later. You'll probably become conditioned to complete your assignments more quickly, and you'll lessen the risk of leaving other, perhaps more important, work unfinished.

"I'm Allergic to My Desk"

There's nothing wrong with your study area. It's in a quiet corner of the house with few distractions. It's well-lit, well-ventilated, and all your materials are within reach. But... every time you sit down to study, you find yourself coming up with any excuse to leave.

It can happen. You set up the ideal study area, follow your time-management system, and stick to your schedule religiously. Your intentions are good, but, for some reason, something just isn't working. Bad vibes, maybe.

What can you do?

Solution: Change your environment!

Just as you can condition yourself to study, you can also condition yourself not to study in a particular location. Stick to your schedule, but try another area—another room, another floor in the library, even a place that may not seem as conducive to quiet study. Maybe you're one of those people who needs a little music or background activity to concentrate.

If changing your environment doesn't help, consider altering your study behavior. Are you trying to study at a time of day when you're overly energetic? Maybe switching your study time earlier or later would help. Try taking a brisk walk or exercising before you begin studying.

Have you had several cups of coffee (or cans of soda) prior to your study period? Caffeine overdose—or too much sugar and caffeine—could make it very difficult to concentrate.

Here's another trick: Select a symbol that you can associate with studying, such as a hat, a scarf, even one of those little trolls people keep on their desks. Whenever it's time to study, just jam on the hat, wrap yourself in the scarf, or set the troll prominently on your desk. It's study time! Not only will this "get you in the mood" to study, it will serve as a warning to roommates, friends, or family members that you are working.

Don't associate your new "study symbol" with anything but studying. Don't wear your study hat to baseball games or leave your troll on the desk while you're on the phone with friends. The instant your study symbol is associated with something other than studying, it begins to lose its effectiveness as a study aid.

A Conspiracy to Keep You from Stuyding

Friends and family call when you're studying because they know that's the best time to reach you at home. Or you're interrupted by phone calls for family members or roommates. Worse yet are the calls from people taking surveys, asking for donations, or trying to sell you something.

Solution: A ringing phone is virtually impossible to ignore. Even if you're determined not to pick it up, it still demands your attention. Voice mail or an answering machine will eliminate you from getting roped into lengthy conversations, but your train of thought will still be interrupted. Turn off the ringer or unplug the phone and let your voice mail take calls while you're studying. Or remove yourself from within hearing distance—go to the library or a friend's house.

A Little Help from Your "Friends"

Your roommate, whose study hours differ from yours, always seems to want to spend "quality bonding time" in the middle of your heavy-duty reading assignments.

Solution: It's not rude to refuse to talk to someone while you're studying, but it often feels like it is. A favorite tip from human relations specialists is to respond in a positive but diverting way such as "It sounds like this is important to you. I really want to hear more. Can we talk in an hour when I'm done with this, so I can concentrate more on your problem?" (Granted, your roommate will consider you uber-geeky if you actually talk like this. Put it in your own words—it's the attitude that's important.)

Another solution might be to put up a "Do Not Disturb" sign, indicating the time you will be available to talk. This will alert others before they unintentionally interrupt you.

You Can't Count on Anyone

You painstakingly plan your schedule each week, religiously keeping track of every appointment, assignment, and commitment you have. Unfortunately, others don't seem to have the same sense of responsibility. Your friends cancel social engagements, you arrive on time for a meeting and no one else shows up, and your teacher even postpones the pretest study session.

Solution: Yes, it's time for another attitude adjustment. Welcome to the real world!

First of all, there's really nothing you can do when some-one else cancels or postpones a scheduled appointment. Occasional—and sometimes more than occasional—cancellations, postponements, or reschedulings should not ruin your schedule...or your day.

Try looking at such last-minute changes as opportunities. Your doctor canceled your appointment? That means a free hour to get ahead in calculus, read your history assignment, work out at the gym...or just do nothing!

Old Habits Die Hard

As you begin to implement your own organizational system for success, you may need to rid yourself of some old habits:

1. **Don't make your schedule overly vague.** When you're scheduling your time, be specific about which tasks you plan to do, when you plan to do them, and how long you think each will take.

2. **Don't delay your planning.** It's easy to convince yourself that you will plan the details of a particular task when the time comes. But that makes it much too easy to forget your homework when your friends invite you to go to the park or out for a snack.

3. **Write everything down.** Not having to remember assignments, due dates, appointments, and schedules will free up space in your brain for the things you need to concentrate on or have to remember. As a general rule, write down the so-called little things and you'll avoid data overload and clutter.

4. Learn to manage distractions. Don't respond to the urgent and forget the important. It's easy to become distracted when the phone rings, your baby brother chooses to trash your room, or you realize your favorite TV show is coming on. But don't just drop your books and run off. Take a few seconds to make sure you have reached a logical stopping point. The time it will take to get your head back on track when you're ready to resume studying is time wasted.

5. Keep a reminder pad on your desk. If you suddenly think of something important, jot it down...then go right back to the assignment you were working on. And if you find yourself day dreaming about something other than what you're studying, write yourself a note or two about it, then get right back to studying.

6. Don't "shotgun" plan. Even if you haven't been following a systematic time-management approach, you may have had some way of keeping important dates and events in mind. Some students use what might be called the "shotgun" approach—writing down assignments, dates, and times on whatever is available. They wind up with so many slips of paper in so many places, their planning attempts are virtually worthless. Record all upcoming events and tasks on your daily and long-term calendars. And always have your daily calendar with you so you can refer to it when you need to add an appointment or assignment.

7. Don't "over-schedule." As you begin to follow a
time-management program, you may find yourself
trying to schedule too much of your time. Once you
get the "effectiveness bug" and become aware of how
much you can accomplish, it might be tempting to
squeeze more and more into your life. Be careful:
Over-scheduling is the biggest reason students
discard a time-management system.

8. Be honest with yourself when estimating how
long assignments will take and your ability to complete them to your satisfaction in the time available.
Chances are you can't complete an outline for your
English term paper, study three chapters of biology,
and do your French assignment in the 40 minutes
you have between class and work. Schedule enough
time to get each assignment done. Whenever possible,
schedule pleasurable activities after study time,
not before. They will then act as incentives, not
distractions.

9. Remember that time is relative. Car trips take
longer if you have to schedule frequent stops for gas,
food, necessities, etc.—longer still if you start out
during rush hour. And everything will take longer if
you consistently tackle the most complex projects
when you're most tired and, therefore, least
productive.

10. **Be prepared.** As assignments are entered into your calendar, make sure you also enter items required to complete them—texts; other books you have to buy, borrow, or get from the library; special materials; etc. There's nothing worse than sitting down to do that assignment you've put off until the last minute and realizing that you're finally ready to get to work, but your supplies aren't...and at 10 p.m., you don't have a lot of options!

11. **Be realistic.** Plan according to your schedule, your goals, and your aptitudes, not some ephemeral "standard." Allocate the time you expect a project to take you, not the time it might take someone else or how long your teacher tells you it should take.

12. **Be flexible, monitor, and adjust.** No calendar is an island. Any new assignment will affect whatever you've already scheduled. If you have a reasonably light schedule when a new assignment suddenly appears, it can just be plugged right into your calendar and finished as scheduled. But if you've already planned virtually every hour for the next two weeks, any addition may force you to change a whole day's plan. Be flexible and be ready. It'll happen.

13. **Look for more time savings.** If you find that you are consistently allotting more time than necessary to a specific chore—giving yourself 1 hour to review your English notes every Sunday but always finishing in 45 minutes or less—change your future schedule accordingly.

14. **Accomplish one task before going on to the next one.** Don't skip around.

15. **Do your least favorite chores** (study assignments, projects, whatever) first. You'll feel better having gotten them out of the way!

16. **Try anything that works.** You may decide that color coding your calendar—red for assignments that must be accomplished that week, blue for steps in longer term projects, yellow for personal time and appointments, green for classes, etc.— helps you stay on schedule. Okay, go ahead. (But if you're spending more time on your coloring than the assignments due tomorrow, you may want to reevaluate your decision.)

17. **Adapt these tools to your own use.** Try anything you think may work—use it if it does, discard it if it doesn't.

There are thinkers and there are doers.

And there are those who think a lot about doing.

Organizing your life requires you to actually use the tools we've discussed, not just waste more time "planning" instead of studying!

Planning is an ongoing learning process. Dive in and plan for your upcoming school term. Or if you're in the middle of a term or semester, plan the remainder of it right now. As you use your plan in the upcoming weeks and months, you will inevitably find your own creative ways to improve your time-management system and tailor it to your own needs.

Chapter 6

Get Organized
for Class

M ost students either take too many notes or too few.

Many of you will develop severe cases of carpal-tunnel syndrome in crazed efforts to reproduce every single word your teachers utter.

Others take notes so sparse that when they review them weeks—or merely hours—later, their scratches make so little sense they might as well have been etched in Sanskrit.

If you feel compelled to take down your teacher's every pearly word, or recopy your entire text, you certainly won't have much of a social life—where would you find the time? Maybe you're so horrified at the prospect of reliving those hours of lectures and chapters of text that you simply never review your notes. And if you avoid taking any notes...well, I don't need to tell you what kind of grades you should expect.

Taking notes should be the ultimate exercise in good old American pragmatism. Take notes only on the material that helps you develop a thorough understanding of your subject...and get good grades. And do it in a way that is, first and foremost, useful and understandable to you. A method that's easy to use would be a real plus.

Taking effective notes requires five separate actions on your part:

1. Listening actively.

2. Selecting pertinent information.

3. Condensing it.

4. Sorting/organizing it.

5. Interpreting it (later).

Most students have a difficult time developing a good note-taking technique and recognizing the information that always shows up on tests—an understanding of which is essential for good grades.

Failing to learn good note-taking methods, they resort to what I think are useless substitutes, like tape recorders.

Know Your Teacher

First and foremost, you must know and understand the kind of teacher you've got and his likes, dislikes, preferences, style, and what he expects you to get out of the class. Depending on your analysis of your teacher's habits, goals, and tendencies, preparation may vary quite a bit, whatever the topic or format of the class.

Take something as simple as asking questions during class, which I encourage you to do whenever you don't understand a key point. Some teachers are very confident fielding questions at any time during a lesson; others prefer questions to be held until the end of the day's lesson; still others discourage questions (or any interaction for that matter) entirely. Learn when and how each one of your teachers likes to field questions, then ask them accordingly.

No matter how ready a class is to enter into a freewheeling discussion, some teachers fear losing control and veering away from their very specific lesson plan. Such teachers may well encourage discussion but always try to steer it into a predetermined path (their lesson plan). Other teachers thrive on chaos, in which case you can never be sure what's going to happen.

Approaching a class with the former type of teacher should lead you to participate as much as possible in the class discussion, but warn you to stay within whatever boundaries she has obviously set.

Getting ready for a class taught by the latter kind of teacher requires much more than just reading the text— there will be a lot of emphasis on your understanding key concepts, interpretation, analysis, and your ability to apply those lessons to cases never mentioned in your text at all!

In general, the rest of this chapter outlines how you should prepare for any class before you walk through the door and take your seat.

Complete All Assignments

Regardless of a particular teacher's style or the classroom format she is using, virtually every course you take will have a formal text (or two or three or more) assigned to it. Though the way the text explains or covers particular topics may differ substantially from your teacher's approach to the same material, your text is still the basis of the course and a key ingredient in your studying. You must read it, plus any other assigned books, before you get to class.

You may sometimes feel you can get away without reading assigned books beforehand, especially in a lecture format where you know the chances of being called on are slim to none. But fear of being questioned on the material is certainly not the only reason to read it. You will be lost if the professor decides—for the first time ever!—to spend the entire period asking the students questions. I've had it happen. And it was not a pleasant experience for the unprepared.

You'll also find it harder to take clear and concise notes in class when you don't know what's in the text— in which case you'll be frantically taking notes on material you could have underlined in your books the night before. You'll also find it difficult to evaluate the relative importance of the teacher's remarks.

Remember: Completing your reading assignment includes not just reading the main text but any other books or articles assigned, plus handouts that may have been previously passed out. It also means completing any nonreading assignments—turning in a lab report, preparing a list of topics, or being ready to present your oral report.

Needless to say, while doing your homework is important, turning it in is an essential second step! My daughter Lindsay refused to use any organizational system for a short time. As a result, in addition to a host of missed appointments and forgotten assignments, she would often forget to pack the homework she did do, or bring it to school but forget to turn it in.

One simple change I made in her routine has made a world of difference: She now has a bright red manila folder, marked "HOMEWORK," into which she puts every completed assignment the instant it's done. When she gets to class, she immediately pulls out her folder to see if she has something to turn in. (She's also given up on her "nonorganizational" system, but that's another story.)

Review Your Notes

Both from your reading and from the previous class. Your teacher is probably going to start this lecture or discussion from the point he left off last time. And you probably won't remember where that point was from week to week...unless you check your notes.

Have Questions Ready

Go over your questions before class. That way, you'll be able to check off the ones the lecturer or teacher answers along the way and only ask those left unanswered.

Prepare Required Materials

Come to class with your notebook, text, pens or pencils, and other such basics, plus particular class requirements like a calculator, drawing paper, or other books.

Learn "Selective" Listening

Taking concise, clear notes is first and foremost the practice of discrimination—developing your ability to separate the essential from the superfluous, to identify and retain key concepts, key facts, and key ideas, and ignore the rest. In turn, this requires the ability to listen to what your teacher is saying and write down only what you need to understand the concept. For some, that could mean a single sentence. For others, a detailed example will be key.

Remember: The quality of your notes usually has little to do with their length—three key lines that reveal the core concepts of a whole lecture are far more valuable than paragraphs of less important data.

So why do some people keep trying to take verbatim notes, convinced that the more pages they cover with scribbles the better students they're being? It's probably a sign of insecurity—they may not have read the material or have a clue about what's being discussed, but at least they'll have complete notes!

Even if you find yourself wandering helplessly in the lecturer's wake, so unsure of what she's saying that you can't begin to separate the important, noteworthy material from the nonessential verbiage, use the techniques discussed in this book to organize and condense your notes anyway.

If you really find yourself so lost that you are just wasting your time, consider adding a review session to your schedule (to read or reread the appropriate texts) and, if the lecture or class is available again at another time, attend again. Yes, it is, strictly speaking, a waste of your precious study time, but not if it's the only way to learn and understand important material.

Take Notes About What You Don't Know

You know the first line of the Gettysburg Address. You know the chemical formula for water. You know what date Pearl Harbor was bombed. So why waste time and space writing them down?

Frequently, your teachers will present material you already know in order to set the stage for further discussion or to introduce material that is more difficult. Don't be so conditioned to automatically copy down dates, vocabulary terms, formulas, and names that you mindlessly take notes on information you already know. You'll just be wasting your time— both in class and later, when you review your overly detailed notes.

This is why some experts recommend that you bring your notes or outline of your textbook reading to class and add your class notes to them. I think it's an effective way to easily organize all your notes for that class, even if it effectively kills the idea of highlighting or underlining your text.

Observe Your Instructor's Style

All instructors (perhaps I should say all effective instructors) develop a plan of attack for each class. They decide what points they will make, how much time they will spend reviewing assignments and previous lessons, what texts they will refer to, what anecdotes they will use to provide comic relief or human interest, and how much time they'll allow for questions.

Building a note-taking strategy around each instructor's typical plan of attack for lectures is another key to academic success.

Throughout junior high school and much of high school, I had to struggle to get good grades. I took copious notes, studied them every night, and pored over them before every quiz and exam.

I was rewarded for my efforts with straight As, but resented the hours I had to put in while my less ambitious buddies found more intriguing ways to spend their time.

But some of the brighter kids had leisure time, too. When I asked them how they did it, they shrugged their shoulders and said they didn't know.

These students had an innate talent that they couldn't explain, a sixth sense about what to study, what were the most important things a teacher said, and what instructors were most likely to ask about on tests.

In fact, if I raised a particular worry, they would say, "Oh, she'll never ask us about that." And sure enough, she never did.

What's more, these students had forgotten many of the details I was sweating. They hadn't even bothered to write any of them down, let alone try to remember them.

What these students innately knew was that items discussed during any lesson could be grouped into several categories, which varied in importance:

- Information not contained in the class texts and other assigned readings.

- Explanations of obscure material covered in the texts and readings but with which students might have difficulty.

- Demonstrations or examples that provided greater understanding of the subject matter.

- Background information that put the course material in context.

As you are listening to an instructor, decide which of these categories best describes the information being presented to you. This will help to determine how detailed your notes on the material should be. (This will become especially easy as some time passes and you get to know the instructor.)

Read, Read, Read

Most good instructors will follow a text they've selected for the course. Likewise, unless they've written the textbook themselves (which you will find surprisingly common in college), most teachers will supplement it with additional information. Good teachers will look for shortcomings in textbooks and spend varying amounts of class time filling in these gaps.

As a result, it makes sense to stay one step ahead of your instructors. Read ahead in your textbook so that, as an instructor is speaking, you know what part of the lesson you should write down and what parts of it are already written down in your textbook. Conversely, you'll immediately recognize the supplemental material on which you might need to take more detailed notes.

Will you be asked about this supplemental material on your exams? Perhaps.

Of course, if you ask your teacher that question, he'll probably say something like, "You are expected to know everything that's mentioned in this class." That's why it's best to pay attention (and not ask stupid questions you already know the answers to!).

You will quickly learn to tell from a teacher's body language what he considers important and what he considers tangential.

In addition, your experience with the teacher's exams and spot quizzes will give you a great deal of insight into what she considers most important.

Sit Near the Front of the Room

Minimize distractions by sitting as close to the instructor as you can.

The farther you sit from the teacher, the more difficult it is to listen. Sitting toward the back of the room means more heads bobbing around in front of you and more students staring out the window—encouraging you to do the same.

Sitting up front has several benefits. You will make a terrific first impression on the instructor—you might very well be the only student sitting in the front row. He'll see immediately that you have come to class to listen and learn, not just take up space.

You'll be able to hear the instructor's voice, and the instructor will be able to hear you when you ask and answer questions.

Finally, being able to see the teacher clearly will help ensure that your eyes don't wander around the room and out the windows, taking your brain with them.

So, if you have the option of picking your desk in class, sit down right in front.

Avoid Distracting Classmates

The gum cracker. The doodler. The practical joker. The whisperer. Even the perfume sprayer. Your classmates may be wonderful friends, entertaining lunch companions, and ultimate weekend party animals, but their quirks, idiosyncrasies, and personal hygiene habits can prove distracting when you sit next to them in class.

Knuckle cracking, giggling, whispering, and note passing are just some of the evils that can divert your attention in the middle of your math professor's discourse on quadratic equations. Avoid them.

Listen for Verbal Clues

Identifying noteworthy material means finding a way to separate the wheat—that which you should write down—from the chaff—that which you should ignore. How do you do that? By listening for verbal clues and watching for the nonverbal ones.

Certainly not all teachers will give you the clues you're seeking. But many will invariably signal important material in the way they present it—pausing (waiting for all the pens to rise), repeating the same point (perhaps even one already made and repeated in your textbook), slowing down their normally supersonic lecture speed, speaking more loudly (or more softly), or even by simply stating, "I think the following is important."

There are also numerous words and phrases that should signal noteworthy material (and, at the same time, give you the clues you need to logically organize your notes): "First of all," "Most importantly," "Therefore," "As a result," "To summarize," "On the other hand," "On the contrary," "The following (number of) reasons (causes, effects, decisions, facts, etc.)."

Such words and phrases give you the clues to not just write down the material that follows, but also to put it in context—to make a list ("First," "The following reasons"); to establish a cause-and-effect relationship ("Therefore," "As a result"); to establish opposites or alternatives ("On the other hand," "On the contrary"); to signify a conclusion ("To summarize," "Therefore"); or to offer an explanation or definition.

Look for Nonverbal Clues

If the teacher begins looking at the window or his eyes glaze over, he's sending you a clear signal: "Put your pen down. This isn't going to be on the test. (So don't take notes!)"

On the other hand, if she turns to write something on the blackboard, makes eye contact with several students, and/or gestures dramatically, she's sending a clear signal about the importance of the point she's making.

Learn how to be a detective—don't overlook the clues.

Ask Questions Often

Being an active listener means asking yourself if you understand everything that has been discussed. If the answer is "no," you must ask the instructor questions at an appropriate time or write down the questions you need answered later.

To Tape or Not to Tape

I am opposed to using a tape recorder in class as a substitute for an active brain for the following reasons:

- **It's time consuming.** To be cynical, not only will you have to waste time sitting in class, you'll have to waste more time listening to that class again!
- **It's virtually useless for review.** Fast-forwarding and rewinding cassettes to find the salient points of a lecture is torture. During the hectic days before an exam, do you really want to waste time listening to a whole lecture when you could just reread your notes?

- **It offers no backup.** Only the most diligent students record and take notes. What happens if your tape recorder malfunctions? How useful will blank or distorted tapes be when it's review time?
- **It costs money.** Compare the price of blank paper and a pen to that of a recorder, batteries, and tapes. The cost of batteries alone should convince you that you're better off going the low-tech route.
- **You miss the "live" clues we discussed earlier.** When all you have is a tape, you don't see that flash in your teacher's eyes, passionate arm flailing, or stern set of the jaw, any and all of which scream, "Pay attention. This will be on your test!"

Create Your Own Shorthand

You don't have to be a master of shorthand to streamline your note taking. Here are five ways:

1. **Eliminate vowels.** As a sign that was ubiquitous in the New York City subways used to proclaim, "If u cn rd ths, u cn gt a gd jb." (If you can read this, you can get a good job.) And, we might add, "u cn b a btr stdnt."

2. **Use word beginnings** ("rep" for representative, "Con" for Congressperson) and other easy-to-remember abbreviations.

3. **Stop putting periods after all abbreviations.** They add up!

4. **Create your own symbols** and abbreviations based on your needs and comfort level.

There are three specific symbols I think you'll want to create—they'll be needed again and again:

W That's my symbol for "What?" as in "What the heck does that mean?"; "What did she say?"; or "What happened? I'm completely lost!" It denotes something that's been missed—leave space in your notes to fill in the missing part of the puzzle after class.

M That's my symbol for "My thought." I want to separate my thoughts during a lecture from the professor's—put too many of your own ideas (without noting they're yours) and your notes begin to lose serious value!

T! My symbol for "Test!" as in "I'm betting the farm this point is probably on the test, so don't forget to review it!!!"

5. **Use standard symbols** in place of words. The list on the following page, some of which you may recognize from math or logic courses, may help you.

While I recommend using the "common" symbols and abbreviations listed on the next page all the time, in every class in order to maintain consistency, you may want to create specific symbols or abbreviations for each class. In chemistry, "TD" may stand for thermodynamics and "K" for the Kinetic Theory of Gases (but don't mix it up with the "K" for Kelvin). In history, "GW" is the father of our country, "ABE" is Mr. Honesty, "FR" could be French Revolution, and "IR" is the Industrial Revolution.

How do you keep everything straight? Create a list on the first page of that class's notebook or binder section for the abbreviations and symbols you intend to use regularly throughout the semester.

≈	approximately
w/	with
w/o	without
wh/	which
→	resulting in
←	as a result of/consequence of
+	and or also
*	most importantly
cf	compare; in comparison; in relation to
ff	following
<	less than
>	more than
=	the same as
↑	increasing
↓	decreasing
esp	especially
Δ	change
⊂	it follows that
∴	therefore
b/c	because

Expanding on Your "Shorthand"

Continue to abbreviate more as additional terms become readily recognizable—in that way, the speed and effectiveness of your note taking will increase as the school year grinds on.

Many students are prone to write big when they are writing fast and to use only a portion of the width of their paper. I guess they figure that turning over pages quickly means they are taking great notes. All it really means is that they are taking notes that will be difficult to read or use when it's review time.

Force yourself to write small and take advantage of the entire width of your paper. The less unnecessary movement, the better.

The Cornell System

Here's a well-known note-taking system many college students are taught. If it works for you, use it.

Start by drawing a vertical line two to three inches from the left side of your notebook paper. Take notes to the right of this line.

During the lecture: Take notes as you normally would—in paragraph form, outline, or using your own shorthand.

After the lecture: Reread your notes and reduce them to the key words that will help you recall the important points of the lecture. Write those key words and phrases in the left column. As you get better at this, you will find that reviewing for a test will only require studying the left column—short and concise—not the right.

What To Do After Class

As soon as possible after your class, review your notes, fill in the "blanks," mark down questions you need to research in your text or ask during the next class, and remember to mark any new assignments on your weekly calendar.

I tend to discourage recopying your notes as a general practice, since I believe it's more important to work on taking good notes the first time around and not wasting the time it takes to recopy. But if you tend to write fast and illegibly, it might also be a good time to rewrite your notes so they're readable, taking the opportunity to summarize as you go. The better your notes, the better your chance of capturing and recalling the pertinent material.

It is not easy for most high school students to do so, but in college, where you have a greater say in scheduling your classes, I recommend "one period on, one off"—an open period, even a half hour, after each class to review that class's notes and prepare for the next one.

If you find yourself unable to take full advantage of such in-between time, schedule as little time between classes as you can.

Are You Among the Missing?

Even if you diligently apply all of the tips in this chapter, it will all be moot if you regularly miss class. So don't! It's especially important to attend all classes near semester's end. Teachers sometimes use the last week to review the entire semester (what a great way to minimize your own review time!), clarify specific topics they feel might still be fuzzy, or answer questions. Students invariably ask about the final exam during this period, and some teachers virtually outline what's going to be on the test!

If you must miss a class, find that verbatim note taker who hasn't followed my advice and borrow her notes. That way, you get to decide what's important enough to copy down. (Some professors might even lend you their notes. It's worth asking!)

Chapter 7

Organize Your Reading and Writing

Making effective notes from your texts should:

- Help you recognize the most important points of a text.
- Make it easier for you to understand those important points.
- Enhance your memory of the text.
- Provide a highly efficient way to study for your exams.

Go for the Gold, Ignore the Pyrite

Step one in effective note taking from texts is to write down the principal points the author is trying to make.

These main ideas should be placed either in the left-hand margin of your notepaper or as headings. Do not write complete sentences.

Then, write down the most important details or examples the author uses to support each of these arguments. These details should be noted under their appropriate main idea. I suggest indenting them and writing each idea on a new line, one under the other. Again, do not use complete sentences. Include only enough details so that your notes are not "Greek to you" when you review them.

I'm sure it's abundantly clear to all of you that not many best-selling authors moonlight writing textbooks. Most of the tomes given to you in classes—even the ones for literature classes—are poorly written, badly organized cures for insomnia. Dull is the kindest word to describe all too many of them.

That said, it's also clear that no matter how dull the prose, your job is to mine the important details from your textbooks so you get good grades. Lest you have to wade through that lifeless mass of words more than once, why not take great notes the first time through?

You can borrow many of the strategies you implement for taking notes in class for your attack on your reading assignments. Just as you use your active brain to listen carefully to what your teacher talks about, you can use that same piece of equipment to read actively:

- Read, then write.
- Make sure you understand the big picture.
- Take notes on what you don't know.

Change the Way You Read

When we read books for pleasure, we tend to read, naturally, from the beginning to the end. (Though some of us may be guilty of taking a peek at the last chapter of a suspenseful mystery novel.) Yet this linear approach, beginning at point A and moving in a direct manner to point B, is not necessarily the most effective way to read texts for information.

If you find yourself plowing diligently through your texts without having the faintest clue as to what you've read, it's time to change the way you read. The best students don't wade through each chapter of their textbooks from beginning to end. Instead, they read in an almost circular fashion. Here's how.

Look for Clues

If we're curled up with the latest Stephen King thriller, we fully expect some clues along the way that will hint at the gory horror to come. And we count on Agatha Christie to subtly sprinkle keys to her mysteries' solutions long before they are resolved in the drawing room.

But most of you probably never tried to solve the mysteries of your own textbooks by using the telltale signs almost all of them contain. That's right: Textbooks are riddled with clues that will reveal to the perceptive student all the noteworthy material that must be captured. Here's where to find them.

Chapter heads and subheads. Bold-faced headings and subheadings announce the detail about the main topic. And in some textbooks, paragraph headings or bold-faced lead-ins announce that the author is about to provide finer details. So start each reading assignment by going through the chapter, beginning to end, reading only the bold-faced heads and subheads.

Knowing what the author is driving at in a textbook will help you look for the important building blocks for her conclusions while you're reading. This will make you a much more active reader.

Pictures, graphs, and charts. Most textbooks, particularly those in the sciences, will have charts, graphs, numerical tables, maps, and other illustrations. All too many students see these as mere fillers—padding to glance at, then forget.

If you're giving these charts and graphs short shrift, you're really shortchanging yourself. You don't have to redraw the tables in your notes, but observe how they supplement the text and what points they emphasize, and make note of these. This will help you put them into your own words, which will help you remember them later. And it will ensure that you don't have to continually refer to your textbooks when brushing up for an exam.

Highlighted terms, vocabulary, and other facts. In some textbooks, you'll discover that key terms and other such information are highlighted within the body text. (And I don't mean by a previous student; consider such yellow-swathed passages with caution—their value is directly proportional to that student's final grade, which you don't know.) Whether boldface, italic, or boxed, this is usually an indication that the material is noteworthy.

Questions. Some textbook publishers use a format in which key points are emphasized by questions, either within the body of the text or at the end of the chapter. If you read these questions before reading the chapter, you'll have a better idea of the answers you should be searching for.

These standard organizational tools should make your reading job simpler. The next time you have to read a history, geography, or similar text, try skimming the assigned pages first. Read the heads, the subheads, and the call-outs. Read the first sentence of each paragraph. Then go back and start reading the details.

To summarize the skimming process:

1. Read and be sure you understand the title or heading. Try rephrasing it as a question for further clarification of what you will read.

2. Examine all the subheadings, illustrations, and graphics—these will help you identify the significant matter within the text.

3. Read thoroughly the introductory paragraphs, the summary, and any questions at chapter's end.

4. Read the first sentence of every paragraph—this generally includes the main idea.

5. Evaluate what you have gained from this process: Can you answer the questions at the end of the chapter? Could you intelligently participate in a class discussion on the material?

6. Write a brief summary that illustrates what you have learned from your skimming.

7. Based on this evaluation, decide whether a more thorough reading is required.

Now for the Fine Print

Now that you have gotten a good overview of the contents by reading the heads and subheads, reviewing the summary, picking up on the highlighted words and information, and considering the review questions that may be included, you're finally ready to read the chapter.

If a more thorough reading is required, turn back to the beginning. Read one section (chapter, etc.) at a time. And do not go on to the next until you've completed the following exercise:

1. Write definitions of any key terms you feel are essential to understanding the topic.

2. Write questions and answers you feel clarify the topic.

3. Write any questions for which you don't have answers—then make sure you answer them by rereading, further research, or asking another student or your teacher.

4. Even if you still have unanswered questions, move on to the next section and complete numbers one to three for that section. (And so on, until your reading assignment is complete.)

See if this method doesn't help you get a better handle on any assignment right from the start.

Because you did a preliminary review first, you'll find that your reading will go much faster.

But...don't assume that now you can speed through your reading assignment. Don't rush through your textbook, or you'll just have to read it again.

Sure, we've all heard about the boy and girl wonders who can whip through 1,000 or even 2,000 words per minute and retain everything, but most of us will never read that fast. That's fine—it's better to read something slowly and remember it than rush it into oblivion. Many great students—even those in law school or taking umpteen courses on the 19th-century novel—never achieve reading speeds even close to 1,000 words per minute. Some of them have to read passages they don't understand again and again to get the point. There's nothing wrong with that.

The most intelligent way to read is with comprehension, not speed, as your primary goal.

Many students underline portions of their textbooks or use magic markers to "highlight" them; however, I am not a great fan of this practice. Highlighting may help certain of you remember the highlighted information, but only at the expense of other information. It is not helpful and, in fact, is far more trouble than it's worth if the material is too dense or too complicated. Highlighting is so limited in effectiveness, I would simply suggest that those of you who still use it, stop.

Others write notes in the margin. This is a little bit better as a strategy for getting higher grades, but marginalia usually make the most sense only in context, so this messy method also forces the student to reread a great deal of text.

What's the most effective way to read and remember your textbooks?

The Importance of Outlining

Outlining a textbook, article, or other secondary source is a little bit like what the Japanese call "reverse engineering"— a way of developing a diagram for something so that you can see exactly how it's been put together. Seeing how published authors build their arguments and marshal their research will help you when it comes time to write your own papers.

Seeing that logic of construction will also help you a great deal in remembering the book—by putting the author's points down in your words, you will be building a way to retrieve the key points of the book more easily from your memory.

What's more, outlining will force you to distinguish the most important points from those of secondary importance, helping you build a true understanding of the topic.

Do Like the Romans Do

Standard outlines use Roman numerals (I, II, III, IV), capital letters (A, B, C, D), Arabic numerals (1, 2, 3, 4), lowercase letters (a, b, c, d), and indentations to illustrate the relationship and importance of topics in the text. While you certainly don't have to use the Roman numeral system, your outline should be organized in the following manner:

Title

Author

I. First important topic in the text

    A. First subtopic

        1. First subtopic of A

           a. First subtopic of 1

           b. Second subtopic of 1

        2. Second subtopic of A

II. The second important topic in the text

Get the idea? In a book, the Roman numerals would usually refer to chapters, the capital letters to subheadings, and the Arabic numbers and lowercase letters to blocks of paragraphs. In an article or single chapter, the Roman numerals would correspond to subheadings, capital letters to blocks of paragraphs, Arabic numerals to paragraphs, and small letters to key sentences.

The discipline of creating outlines will help you zero in on the most important points an author is making and capture them, process them, and, thereby, retain them.

Sometimes an author will put the major point of a paragraph in the first sentence. But just as often, the main idea of a paragraph or section will follow some of these telltale words: therefore, because, thus, since, as a result.

When you see these words, you should identify the material they introduce as the major points in the outline. The material immediately preceding and following almost always will be in support of these major points. The outline is an extraordinary tool for organizing your thoughts and time.

Create a Timeline

I always found it frustrating to read textbooks in social studies. I'd go through chapters on France and the Far East, and have a fairly good understanding of those areas, but no idea where certain events stood in a global context. As more and more colleges add multicultural curricula, you may find it even more difficult to "connect" events in 17th-century France or 19th-century Africa with what was happening in the rest of the world (let alone the U.S.).

An excellent tool for overcoming that difficulty is a timeline that you can update periodically. It will help you visualize the chronology and remember the relationship of key world events.

A simple, abridged timeline of James Joyce's literary life would look like this (I suggest you create a horizontal timeline, but the layout of this book makes reproducing it that way difficult, so here's a vertical version):

1882 Birth

1907 *Chamber Music*

1914 *Dubliners*

1916 *A Portrait of the Artist as a Young Man*

1918   *Exiles*

1922   *Ulysses*

1927   *Pomes Pennyeach*

1937   *Collected Poems*

1939   *Finnegan's Wake*

1941   Death

This makes it easy to see that he was born as the U.S. experienced a post-Civil War boom in industry and population growth and died at the beginning of World War II. If you added information about other literary figures from the same period, you would not soon forget that Joyce, Virginia Woolf, Ezra Pound, W.B. Yeats, Lady Augusta Gregory, Charles Darwin, George Eliot, and D.H. Lawrence, among many others, were all contemporaries. Adding data about nonliterary events to your timeline would enable you to make connections between these authors, their works, and what was going on in the United States, Britain, Europe, Africa, etc.

Draw a Concept Tree

Another terrific device for limiting the amount of verbiage in your notes and making them more memorable is the concept tree. Like a timeline, the concept tree is a visual representation of the relationship among several key facts.

After all "A picture is worth a thousand words," so timelines and concept trees will be much more helpful than mere words in remembering material, particularly conceptual material. For instance, one might depict categories and specific types of animals in this way:

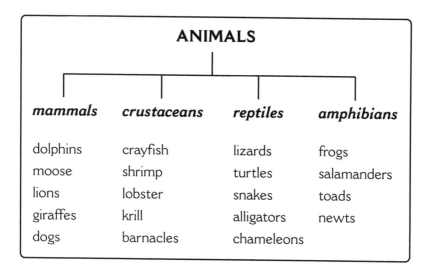

Add a Vocabulary List

Many questions on exams require students to define the terminology in a particular discipline. Your physics professor will want to know what vectors are, your calculus teacher will want to know about differential equations, your history professor will want you to be well-versed on the Cold War, and your English literature professor will require you to know about the Romantic Poets.

As you read your textbook, be sure to write down all new terms that seem important and their definitions. I used to draw a box around terms and definitions in my notes, because I knew these were among the most likely items to be asked about, and the box would always draw my attention to them when I was reviewing.

Wait, You're Not Done Yet

After you've finished taking notes on a chapter, go through them and identify the most important points, either with an asterisk or a highlighter. You'll probably end up marking about 40 to 50 percent of your entries. When you're reviewing for a test, you should read all of the notes, but your asterisks will indicate which points you considered the most important while the chapter was very fresh in your mind.

To summarize, when it comes to taking notes from your texts or other reading material, you should:

- Take a cursory look through the chapter before you begin reading. Look for subheads, highlighted terms, and summaries at the end of the chapter to give you a sense of the content.

- Read each section thoroughly. While your review of the chapter "clues" will help you understand the material, you should read for comprehension rather than speed.

- Take notes immediately after you've finished reading, using the outline, timeline, concept tree, and vocabulary list methods of organization as necessary.

- Mark with an asterisk or highlight the key points as you review your notes.

Notes of Your Research

Sometime during your high school or college years, you will undoubtedly be called upon to do some extensive research, either for a term paper or some other major project. Such a task will indeed be a major undertaking. Note taking will be only one aspect of the process, albeit an important one.

(While I will give you a terrific system for taking notes for a term paper or report in this chapter, I urge you also to read *Improve Your Writing*. It thoroughly covers all the important steps, from selecting a topic and developing an outline, to researching and taking notes, to writing, rewriting, and proofreading your final paper.)

As you will discover, writing a term paper will require you to take notes from a number of sources. So you'll definitely want a note-taking system that is quick, thorough, efficient, and precludes the necessity of having to return to any sources again. What's the answer?

A Great Indexing System

Index cards will cut the time it takes to research and organize a term paper in half.

Here's how they work.

Developing a preliminary outline is an important early step in the paper-writing process. Assuming you have completed this step, you would then be prepared to gather information for your term paper or research project. Proceed to your local office supply store and buy a pack of 3 × 5 note cards.

As you review each source, you'll discover some are packed with helpful information, while others may have no useful material at all. Once you determine that you will use a source, make a working bibliography card:

- **In the upper right corner of the card:** Write the library call number (Dewey decimal or Library of Congress number), or any other detail that will help you locate the material ("Science Reading Room,"

"Main Stacks, 3rd Floor," etc.). If from an online source, carefully copy the full URL address.

- **On the main part of the card:** Write the author's name, if one is given, last name first. Include the title of the article, if applicable, and write and underline the name of the book, magazine, website, or other publication. Include any other details, such as date of publication, edition, volume number, or page numbers where the article or information was found.

- **In the upper left corner:** Number the card—the card for the first source you plan to use, for example, is #1, the second is #2, and so on. If you accidentally skip a number or end up not using a source for which you've filled out a card, don't worry. It's only important that you assign a different number to each card.

By filling out a card for each source, you have just created your working bibliography—a listing of all your sources that will be an invaluable tool when you have to prepare the final bibliography for your term paper.

Shuffling Cards Is a Good Deal

With index cards, you can organize your list of resources in different ways, just by shuffling the deck.

At some point, you might want to have your list of resources organized in alphabetical order, or separated into piles of resources you've checked and those you haven't. No problem: Just shuffle your cards.

Even with the help of a computer, it would be time consuming to do all of this on paper. The note-card system is neater and more efficient, and that's the key to getting your work done as quickly and painlessly as possible!

A Card Game You Will Win

You've completed your bibliography cards. It's time to take notes. Here's how.

Write one thought, idea, quote, or fact—and only one—on each card. There are no exceptions. If you encounter a very long quote or string of data, you can write on both the front and back of the card, if necessary. But never carry over a note to a second card. If you have an uncontrollable urge to do that, the quote is too long. If you feel that the author is making an incredibly good point, paraphrase it.

Write in your own words. Don't copy material word for word—you may inadvertently wind up plagiarizing when you write. Summarize key points or restate the material in your own words.

Put quotation marks around any material copied verbatim. Sometimes an author makes a point so perfectly, so poetically, you do want to capture it exactly as is. It's fine to do this on a limited basis. But when you do so, you must copy such statements exactly—every sentence, every word, every comma should be precisely as written in the original. And make sure you put quotation marks around this material. Don't rely on your memory to recall, later, what you paraphrased and what you copied verbatim.

Put the number of the corresponding bibliography card in the upper left corner. This is the exact same number you put in the upper left corner of the bibliography card.

Include the page numbers (where you found the information) on the card. You can add this information under the resource number.

Write down the topic numeral or letter that corresponds to your preliminary outline. Let's say you're doing a paper about Vietnam, and the second section, "II," of your preliminary outline is about the French withdrawal in the 1950s. You found an interesting quote from a United States official that refers to this withdrawal. Write down the topic numeral "II" in the upper right corner of your note card.

You might come across interesting quotes or statistics that could add flavor and authority to your term paper, but you're not quite sure where they will fit in. Mark the card with an asterisk [*] or other symbol instead. Later, when you have a more detailed outline, you may discover where it fits.

Give it a headline. Next to the topic numeral or letter, add a brief description of the information on the card. For example, your note card about the French withdrawal may read, "French Withdrawal: U.S. Comments."

As you fill out your note cards, be sure to transfer all information accurately. Always double check names, dates, and other statistics. The beauty of using the note-card system is that, once you've captured the information you need, you should never have to return to any of the sources a second time.

A note of caution here: While this system is terrific for helping you organize your time and your material, don't permit it to hamstring you if you find other interesting material.

As with the other exercises in note taking, the index card system requires you not to be a copyist—you could have used the copy machine for that—but a processor of information.

Constantly ask yourself questions while looking at the source material:

Is the author saying this in such a way that I want to quote her directly, or should I paraphrase the material?

If you decide to paraphrase, you obviously don't have to write down the author's exact verbiage, and, therefore, can resort to some of the note-taking tips discussed earlier. The answer to this question will have a big impact on how much time it takes to fill in each index card.

Does this material support or contradict the arguments or facts of another author?

Whom do I believe? If there is contradictory evidence, should I note it? Can I refute it? If it supports the material I already have, is it interesting or redundant?

Where does this material fit into my outline?

Often, source material won't be as sharply delineated as your plan for the term paper, which is why it is important to place one, and only one, thought on each card. Even though an author might place more than one thought into a paragraph, or even a sentence, you will be able to stick to your organizational guns if you keep your cards close to your outline vest.

You'll Be Superorganized

Before I learned this system in high school, my student life was, quite literally, a mess. I had pages and pages of notes for term papers, but sometimes I was unsure where quotes came from and whether or not they were direct quotes or paraphrases. And organizing the voluminous notes when it came time to put my thoughts in order took longer than the researching and writing.

The card system will save you all of that grief. Writing one thought, idea, or quote per card will eliminate the problems caused when disparate pieces of information appear on the same piece of paper. And writing the number of the source down before doing anything else will help you avoid any problems relating to proper attribution.

When you're ready to do your final outline, all you'll need to do is organize and reorder your cards until you have the most effective flow.

This simple note-card system is, in fact, one that many professional writers—including this one—swear by long after they leave the world of term papers and class reports behind.

INDEX

Notes

Notes

Notes

Notes

About the Author

Ron Fry is a nationally known spokesperson for the improvement of public education and an advocate for parents and students playing an active role in strengthening personal education programs. In addition to being the author of the vastly popular *How to Study Program*, Fry has edited or written more than 30 different titles — resources for optimum student success.

"Helpful for students of all ages from high school and up."
– Small Press Book Review

"These are must-read guides every family should have in its library."
– Library Journal

How to Study Series:

- **How to Study**
- **"Ace" Any Test**
- **Get Organized**
- **Improve Your Memory**
- **Improve Your Writing**
- **Improve Your Reading**

For product information and technology assistance, contact us at

Cengage Learning Customer & Sales Support,
1-800-354-9706.